A PARENTS' GUIDE TO
SPIRITUAL WARFARE

A PARENTS' *Guide to* SPIRITUAL WARFARE

EQUIPPING YOUR KIDS TO WIN THE BATTLE

Leslie Montgomery

CROSSWAY BOOKS

A PUBLISHING MINISTRY OF
GOOD NEWS PUBLISHERS
WHEATON, ILLINOIS

Cover design: Josh Dennis

Cover photo: Getty Images

First printing, 2006

Printed in the United States of America

Library of Congress Cataloging-in-Publication Data
Montgomery, Leslie, 1967–
    A parents' guide to spiritual warfare : equipping your kids to win the battle / Leslie Montgomery.
       p. cm.
ISBN 13: 978-1-58134-771-5
ISBN 10: 1-58134-771-5 (tpb)
    1. Spiritual warfare. 2. Parenting—Religious aspects—Christianity.
3. Child rearing—Religious aspects—Christianity. I. Title
BV4509.5.M62   2006
235'.4085—dc22   2006006278

CH		16	15	14	13	12	11	10	09	08	07	06
15	14	13	12	11	10	9	8	7	6	5	4	3	2	1

To my favorite spiritual warfare partner,
DALLAS
who is passionately faithful to battle on behalf
of all God's children.
Second only to Jesus, you're my hero.

Prepare buckler and shield,
and advance for battle!
Harness the horses;
mount, O horsemen!
Take your stations with your helmets,
polish your spears,
put on your armor!

JEREMIAH 46:3-4

CONTENTS

THANK-YOUS

I've learned some of life's greatest lessons from children. So it seems only natural to thank those who have taught me the most:

Charlene, my precious daughter, who has taught me to laugh.

Paul, my small but wise champion, who has indirectly taught me how to seek God persistently and passionately in the spirit realm.

Kendra Austin, whose honesty before Jesus teaches me transparency, and the rest of the Austin clan who have always loved me unconditionally.

All the girls I counseled who came through the Triangle House at the Nashville YWCA, who taught me through their example that trauma from childhood, trial, and heartache are not license to give way to self-pity.

My nephew Jeremiah, who continues to teach me that faith in God is simple, not a chore, and my niece Abagail, who says, "Auntie Weswee, Jesus in your heart" right when I need to hear it the most.

My grandson, Jonathan, who has taught me to trust even when it's scary, and my grandson, Dallin, whose curiosity teaches me it's okay to ask questions—and to expect sound answers.

To my "kids" who spent two weeks with me in Budapest learning spiritual warfare and who continue to battle alongside their parents on mission fields around the world.

To Elijah Crusade, who has personally taught me how deep, wide, and unconditional the love and forgiveness of Jesus Christ really is. I can't wait to see you!

To Vision National, who is teaching me how to minister to children all over the world, and to my "kids" in Costa Rica—Jonathan and Edina, who are teaching me how to give unselfishly to further the kingdom of Christ.

To Samantha and Elijah Drake, my "new" children in the Lord who are teaching me by example how to accept and love others without boundaries.

I love you all so very much.

INTRODUCTION

The topic of spiritual warfare is a double-edged sword within the church, the Body of Christ. On one side, when taken to an extreme, it gives the impression that there is a demon behind every bush, waiting to attack innocent bystanders at a moment's notice. On the other side of the blade, it is brushed off and not even considered as a legitimate spiritual issue that needs any concern. Both views are wrong.

The Bible points to the necessity of spiritual warfare. First Peter 5:8 warns us, "Your adversary the devil prowls around like a roaring lion, seeking someone to devour." Scripture also points to other significant aspects of the spiritual battle apart from the devil—namely, our flesh (that is, our own desires) and the world. Collectively, we can see clearly that spiritual warfare is a battle against the enemy of our souls, our own desires, and the continual onslaught from a sinful world. To completely ignore or to concentrate solely on only one of these three aspects is to minimize the necessity of warfare and to put ourselves and family members at risk of falling into sin and a web of deceit that will inevitably cause emotional pain and spiritual death.

The Bible's clear warnings on the topic of spiritual warfare are not meant to breed fear but to empower us as God's children and as parents. Nowhere does this battle become more evident than in the lives of children today as they are assaulted twenty-four hours a day from every angle. But we need not succumb to a barrage of attacks or give up when we or our children come face to face with opposition. Instead, we have been given the authority and tools to stand against the Evil One on behalf of ourselves and our families through the One who made it possible to do so: Jesus Christ.

When I became a believer in the fall of 1993, my children, Charlene and Paul, were nine and eight years old respectively. Prior to my conversion, I had engaged in numerous ungodly activities far from my new Christian beliefs. At times it was a difficult transition. As a child, alcoholism, sexual abuse, paganism, and self-hatred were part of my daily reality. They were all aspects of my heritage that had been intricately woven by generations before me. Children learn what they're taught; so it was only natural for me as a budding teen to engage in goddess-worship, cultism, spiritualism, and a hodgepodge of various organized religions, and to pass this ungodly heritage on to my children. When I gave my life to Jesus Christ as my Savior, I rocked my family tree so hard in the spirit realm, it caused a perpetual earthquake in my home. My children rebelled, some of my family disowned me, and others relentlessly mocked my newfound faith. I was totally unprepared spiritually for what was transpiring in my world.

Within a week of my conversion I bought a book at a yard sale written by Dr. Ed Murphy called *The Handbook on Spiritual Warfare*. What seemed like a chance discovery was really God's intervention. I knew even then that the spirit realm existed because I'd grown up indulging in its demonic aspect through cultism and paganism. So to find a book from the biblical perspective was like finding a spiritual pot of gold.

I devoured Dr. Murphy's book in conjunction with the Bible and immediately began intervening in the spirit realm on my own behalf and that of my children. I was a single parent, so it was a battle I waged on my own. I spent hours at night when they were sleeping, kneeling next to their beds, praying silently over them. I spoke out every sin I could think of that I'd unwittingly subjected them to in my unsaved state. I renounced all aspects of my involvement in cultism and earnestly asked the Holy Spirit to fill the void that was created when these curses were broken. My children's hearts slowly changed, and I saw their hearts soften and develop a love for Jesus. But my battle didn't end there.

As Charlene and Paul grew and matured into adolescence, they continually struggled with a combination of their own desires, peer pressure from their friends, and direct assaults from the enemy of their souls. As a result, their faith wavered. I hadn't ceased to intervene for them; so I questioned if God was still listening to me as I interceded on their behalf. That's when the Holy Spirit prompted me to empower them to intervene on their own. It was a light bulb moment. After all, it was natural for me to teach them independent living skills in other areas of their lives—why would it be different spiritually?

The core reality of this entire situation was twofold. First, I came to the knowledge that I am not my children's Savior. Let me explain. As parents we often unwittingly create an environment where we are exalted in our children's eyes. Having respect for one's parents and heeding their advice is an important aspect of healthy growth and development for a child, but if we don't teach them the truth, which is that we will fail them and God won't, we set them up for failure. As a Christian parent, it was important to me that they be able to come to me, share their struggles, pray with me, and allow me to pray for them, but I needed to pass the baton and empower them to do so for themselves, learning that they can place their trust in God himself. This was vital because they would eventually leave home and the spiritual umbrella of safety that a godly parent provides and live life on the front line themselves. I would not always be accessible to them for support and encouragement or be able to hold their hands up when they grew weary, but God would *never* leave them or forsake them. Additionally, my resources for helping them would always be limited, but God's are not.

The second reality was that they had allowed certain strongholds into their lives by succumbing to sin, and thus they were the ones who had to renounce their involvement, repent, and ask the Holy Spirit to reside in place of the stronghold. In other words, *they* let the sin in the doors of their hearts, and *they* had to kick it out. As parents, our children's own will can come against our spiritual intervention. Jesus asked the disabled man at the pool of Bethesda a crucial question when the invalid (meaning weak, sick, ill) asked for healing. He said, "Do you want to be healed?" (John 5:6). The seemingly obvious answer to that question is yes, but not all people want to be healed from the pleasures of sin. That's why Satan is called the *Deceiver*—he misleads us to believe that the sin we are engaged in is fun and pleasurable, not enslaving and leading to death.

Parents are not hopeless in this situation, but we are limited by our children's will. We will discuss this further in a future chapter. My point is that it is vital to give our children the necessary discipleship at an early age. This will help them develop trust and intimacy with their Savior. Thus when they experience conviction they will run into the arms of Jesus rather than running away from him in guilt and shame. Running and hiding from God only breeds more sin.

I wish I could honestly say that both my children have excelled in the areas listed above. In certain aspects they have done very well. In others they still struggle. Although they are both adults now, and one has children of her own, we all continue to apply the biblical tools for combating the brutal attack against our souls. We must remember, though, that spiritual warfare is not a one-day conflict but rather a lifetime battle that we will be engaged in until we die.

I will forever be grateful for discovering Dr. Murphy's book. His work, as well as other books on spiritual warfare, specifically those of friend and colleague Neil Anderson, have helped me see that the spiritual realm not only exists but is active in *everyone's* life. Time and again these books have taken me to God's Word, which clearly states that we are at war against the world, Satan, and our flesh, but that hope is found in Jesus Christ.

The demonic strongholds that gripped me since my childhood have released their grasp on my life. In their place is the peace, love, joy, and freedom available in Christ. As a result I've tried adamantly to teach my children the same principles in the hope that they too will train their children to be warriors on behalf of the army of God. I am blessed that the Lord has called me to share with others how to stand against the forces of evil.

This book is the product of years of intense personal study, experience, and collaboration with other ministry leaders. Its purpose is to equip you to walk in freedom, to intervene on your children's behalf, and to teach them to do the same—creating a spiritual heritage for your future grandchildren and so on.

Many fine parenting books will teach you how to discipline your children, how to raise them as responsible adults, and even how to instill morals into their lives. But none of those things have value if your child falls by the spiritual wayside. As a parent, you have a biblical responsibility to intercede in the lives of your children in the spirit realm and to teach your children how to stand against the fiery darts that assault them twenty-four hours a day. Our children have been born "for such a time as this" (Esther 4:14), and it is our role as parents to equip them for the battle at hand through the saving, intervening, and conquering power found only in Jesus Christ.

THE NECESSITY OF
WARFARE

*For I know the plans I have for you, declares the LORD,
plans for wholeness and not for evil, to give you a future
and a hope.*

JEREMIAH 29:11

Jeremiah 1:5 tells us that before our children were conceived and formed in their mother's womb, God knew them. And Jeremiah 29:11 tells us that God's plans for our children are for good and not for evil, to prosper them and to give them a hope and a future. If that's truly the case, then why do the following statistics paint a very different picture?

• Over the last decade, between 347,000 and 544,000 tenth through twelfth grade students dropped out of school *each year* without successfully completing a high school program.[1]

• Suicide is the third leading cause of death among young people ages fifteen to twenty-four. In 2001, 3,971 suicides were reported in this age group.[2]

• In 1999 law enforcement officers arrested an estimated 2.5 million juveniles.[3]

• One million teenage girls get pregnant each year.[4]

• Seven in ten young offenders in 1997 were convicted for violent offenses.[5]

• By the eighth grade, 52 percent of adolescents have consumed alcohol, 41 percent have smoked cigarettes, and 20 percent have used marijuana.[6]

• Twelve percent of eighth graders, 22 percent of tenth graders, and 28 percent of twelfth graders consider themselves heavy drinkers and have consumed five or more drinks in a row at least once in the past two weeks.[7]

• Twenty percent of youths fifteen to eighteen years old report self-mutilation (without an intent to commit suicide), head banging, repetitive self-biting, skin picking, hair pulling, skin cutting, skin carving, and skin burning.[8]

• Currently it is estimated that adolescents (thirteen- to seventeen-year-olds) account for up to one-fifth of all rapes and one-half of all cases of child molestation committed each year.[9]

• In 1995 youths were involved in 15 percent of all forcible rapes—approximately 18 adolescents per 100,000 were arrested for forcible rape. In the same year, approximately 16,100 adolescents were arrested for sexual offenses excluding rape and prostitution.[10]

• According to the National Youth Suicide Prevention Center in Washington, D.C., every hour of every day approximately 228 teenagers in the U.S. attempt to take their lives.

These are just a few statistics that reflect the glaring problems of today's youth. The biggest tragedy in all this is that there is not much difference between believers and nonbelievers. Violent crimes committed by youths, suicide, self-mutilation, and alcohol and drug abuse are as rampant in Christian homes as in non-Christian homes. *These numbers reflect battles lost in the spirit realm.*

If the Bible is correct (which it is), and if God's plans for our children are good, prosperous, and hopeful (which they are), then why do the statistics regarding our children depict a completely different picture?

We can blame the problems of today's youth on many external influences. Television, peer pressure, accessibility to unhealthy choices, and music are just a few. But the truth be known, *all* external behavior is a proclamation of an internal belief. In other words, while our children's behavior can be influenced externally, the core beliefs that they have about themselves, others, God, Satan, and their purpose in life are what ultimately shape their decision-making process.

Few Christian parents would disagree that their children's faith should be reflected in their choices. Isn't that the way we as parents live our own lives? Our convictions about God and his Word make up the rudder that sets a course to healthy decision-making. The truth is, if we made decisions based solely on our biblical convictions, we'd all live close to perfect lives. The problem that exists, and has existed for thousands of years, is the ever-present sin nature that resides in all of us. We mix our convictions in the same bowl with a sin nature that rages out of control, and that leads to spiritual casualties and fatalities. However, when our convictions are blended with submission to Christ, victory and success will follow.

The first step in preparing for battle and teaching our children to do the same is to honestly evaluate our current spiritual state. We cannot step into spiritual combat without a clear understanding of where we stand in our beliefs about God, his Word, our purpose in life, and Satan. The best way to examine where children stand is to ask them, and that's exactly what George Barna of the Barna Group did. He surveyed thirteen-year-olds nationally in an attempt to assess what they had learned and retained about God during their adolescent years. What he found was both encouraging and startling.

First, the good news:

• Nine out of ten young people consider themselves to be Christian by the age of thirteen, with 32 percent receiving Christ as their Savior between the ages of five and twelve, 4 percent in the thirteen to eighteen age range, and 6 percent in the nineteen plus range.

This research shows us that if our children do not embrace Jesus Christ as their Savior before they reach their teenage years, the chance of their doing so at all is slim. Even more so, it shows that nine out of ten children are being exposed to the gospel of Jesus Christ. That is great news! Further studies aren't as encouraging. They show that these same children's theological beliefs are vague at best, revealing that while we may be good at initially reaching our children, we aren't as efficient in educating them. Three-quarters believe the following:

• The devil does not exist—Satan is just a symbol of evil.

• A good person earns entry into heaven by doing enough good works.

• People are born morally neutral and make a choice as to whether they will become good or bad.

• All of the sacred books from different religious traditions (the Bible, the Koran, the Book of Mormon, and so forth) are merely different expressions of the same spiritual truths and principles.

• Spiritual and moral truths can only be discovered through logic, human reason, and personal experience.

Two-thirds believe the following:

• Praying to deceased saints can have a positive effect on your life.

• The Bible discourages sin but never describes it as an innate disposition.

Half or more contended the following:

• Life either has no meaning, or the meaning is realized through hard work, which produces the resources to enjoy comfort and security.

• There are no absolute standards for morals and ethics.

• Life is either a random series of acts or predetermined, but we have no real say in how our lives unfold.

• When Jesus Christ lived on earth, he committed sins.

• The Bible does not specifically condemn homosexuality.[11]

Maybe you're as shocked about these statistics as I was the first time I read them. I thought to myself, *What are we teaching our children?* But when I dug a little deeper, research showed me that we are teaching them exactly what we as their parents believe! These same core beliefs about God, our purpose, the Bible, and Satan are held by an equal number of adults (sometimes more). The reality is that some of us believe these lies ourselves, and just as we have spiritually dog-paddled through life with our heads barely above water, we have raised like-minded children. *This is a spiritual catastrophe.*

In his book *Transforming Our Children into Spiritual*

Champions, George Barna wisely advises parents about being spiritually fit. "When it comes to raising children to be spiritually mature, the old adage, 'you can't give what you don't have,' is pertinent for millions of families. Most parents proclaim that the spiritual nurturing of their children is their job, but are very happy to let their church shape the child's faith. Unfortunately, no matter how hard a church tries, it is incapable of bringing a child to complete spiritual maturity: that is the job of the family."

I believe you have picked up this book because you want to raise godly children before the Lord. I further believe you love your children and want what's best for them—you want them to succeed in standing against the attacks of the world and Satan, to submit their sin nature and will to God, and to live the life of freedom found only in Jesus Christ. But I want to be honest and up-front with you about the gospel of Jesus Christ and spiritual warfare. If you do not have a firm biblical foundation regarding Jesus Christ, Satan, your purpose, the Bible, and the battle at hand, you will be continually defeated in life (which is external evidence of spiritual defeat) and ultimately will be of little value in helping your children learn the necessary tools to live a life of freedom themselves. Jesus spoke of this very problem in Matthew 7:24-27:

> *Everyone then who hears these words of mine and does them will be like a wise man who built his house on the rock. And the rain fell, and the floods came, and the winds blew and beat on that house, but it did not fall, because it had been founded on the rock. And everyone who hears these words of mine and does not do them will be like a foolish man who built his house on the sand. And the rain fell, and the floods came, and the winds blew and beat against that house, and it fell, and great was the fall of it.*

The first step in helping your child is educating yourself. It is through your example that your children will learn the most. It is through your knowledge and confidence in Christ that the seeds of promise that God has made in his Word will bloom. Evidence of intimacy with Jesus in your own life will breed a desire for spiritual intimacy in the life of your child. When your children see you facing life's challenges from a spiritual standpoint and overcoming those challenges in Christ, they will naturally come to you with questions about how they, too, can overcome. As you taste freedom in your own daily battles, your children will desire to feast on the liberty of Christ also. Additionally, as you stand against the attacks of the enemy and become empowered through Christ, you will share these spiritual triumphs with your kids.

Be prepared, fellow parents, because if your children see that life's challenges are overcoming you, rather than your overcoming them, they will gravitate toward the world's way of coping, which inevitably leads to enslavement and spiritual death. Psalm 103:17 tells us that the Lord's love is with those who fear and honor him in their lives, and that when we as parents walk in his righteousness, his love is handed down not only to our children but to our grandchildren! That's a powerful promise for generations yet to come!

GOD'S DESIRE FOR OUR CHILDREN

I started this chapter with Jeremiah 1:5 and 29:11, which tell us that God knew our children before they were formed in their mother's womb and that he has great plans to give them a hope and a prosperous future. Scripture defines what our children's futures look like when their lives are submitted to him:

• God's Son, Jesus Christ, will be reflected in their lives (Galatians 4:19).

• Our children, whom God refers to as seeds of righteousness, will be delivered from the attacks of Satan (Proverbs 11:21; Matthew 6:13).

• They will have great peace in their lives through the teachings of the Lord (Isaiah 54:13).

• They will develop discernment of good and evil and will have a good conscience (Hebrews 5:14; 1 Peter 3:21).

• They will have knowledge of God's laws engraved in their minds and on their hearts (Hebrews 8:10).

• They will choose companions who are wise, not fools, nor sexually immoral, nor drunkards, nor idolaters, nor slanderers, nor swindlers (Proverbs 13:20; 1 Corinthians 5:11).

• They will remain sexually pure and will keep themselves only for their spouse, asking God for his grace to keep such a commitment (Ephesians 5:3, 31-33).

• They will honor their parents (Ephesians 6:1-3).

God has many more plans for our children outlined in his Word. As you read and share the Bible with your children, write them down together. Doing so will ensure that you both understand God's promises and expectations and know what blessings they can expect to receive in the future as they walk in God's will. The Bible has over thirty thousand promises for believers who walk righteously. It is our job as parents to teach our children by example and through our words how to live according to God's Word. In doing so, we are promised that when our children are grown, they will not turn away from the truth (Proverbs 22:6).

THE TRAINING OF A
WARRIOR CHILD

For not in my bow do I trust,
nor can my sword save me.
But you have saved us from our foes
and have put to shame those who hate us.
In God we have boasted continually,
and we will give thanks to your name forever.

PSALM 44:6-8

The greatest injustice we can do as parents is to teach our children to depend on us wholeheartedly rather than on God. They *must* learn to seek God on their own, and we *must* nudge them, at the appropriate times, out of the proverbial spiritual nest. In anticipation of failure, we must also be ready to swoop down at any given moment to catch a floundering fledgling that is dropping helplessly to the ground below.

Because it's both necessary and vital that you as a parent know how to engage in warfare on behalf of your children, and for your children to know how to defend themselves, from this point forward we will look at both aspects exactly as they are to be developed in the life of a parent and child—from *spiritual* conception.

Spiritual conception occurs when God creates a soul. Romans 8:29 confirms that God knew and chose those who would be his children before the earth was created. Therefore, your children have been handpicked by their Creator to be sanctified (that is, set apart for a special purpose) and to be his children (Jeremiah 1:5). When our Creator sanctified our children, what did he set them apart to do? Romans 8:28-30 gives us the answer: to become Christlike, for the sacred purpose of turning from sin and being cleansed from moral corruption.

> *And we know that for those who love God all things work together for good, for those who are called according to his purpose. For those whom he foreknew he also predestined to be conformed to the image of his Son, in order that he might be the firstborn among many brothers. And those whom he predestined he also called, and those whom he called he also justified, and those whom he justified he also glorified.*

What do we learn from this strategic passage?

1. God *foreknew* our children, meaning that *he chose and knew them before they were formed in their mother's womb.*

2. God *predestined* our children, meaning he decided beforehand that they would be *conformed to Jesus*—that is, they would *come together in the likeness or image* of his Son, Jesus.

3. He *called* our children, perhaps meaning *he named them*, but certainly meaning that he has brought them into his plans for them and is involved in their lives to fulfill that plan.

4. He *justified* our children—that is, *he declared them righteous.*

5. He *glorified* our children, meaning he is making them like himself and will someday give them new bodies that aren't susceptible to sin. John Piper has written: "So in Paul's mind, when he said in Romans 8:30, 'the justified are glorified' he meant, God works to make sure that those whom he justified move from one degree of glory to the next (sanctification) and finally reach perfection with new and glorious bodies like Christ's (Hebrews 12:23; Philippians 3:21). So your progressive sanctification—your becoming like Jesus—is as sure

and as firmly planned and worked by God as is your election and pre-destination and calling and justification and final glory."

We all hope to hear the words found in Matthew 25:21, "Well done, good and faithful servant," but I'd be even more enthralled to hear my Father in heaven say that to my children.

All of these wonderful blessings being said, our children still have a choice to accept Jesus Christ as their Savior and develop intimacy with him or to turn away from these blessings. The setting apart that our Father has done does not take away their free will to choose whom they will serve. Therefore, it is the role of parents to train their children for Christ from the time they know God has asked them to conceive and raise a child.

Once prospective parents know that God has entrusted them with the responsibility of a child, they should begin to pray for intervention in each child's life, development, and purpose. Equally so, they should submit themselves to God's counsel regarding how their hearts can be prepared to raise this gift.

It was a fad several years ago for expectant mothers to read the books of scholars or to play Beethoven or Bach for their child during pregnancy. Research revealed that in doing so a child's intelligence was increased. I cannot name a greater scholar than our Creator himself. Imagine the foundation you'd lay as a parent if you read the Word of God and pray for your unborn child daily, believing in faith that seeds of spiritual development are being planted.

Perhaps you think it is silly to intercede or to fight for a baby who is developing within you or in your mate's womb, but I assure you that Satan does not want another child conceived into a Christian home.

If you think that the enemy of our souls has not taken a special interest in your child, you are mistaken. Consider the direct assault on the life of Jesus after conception (Matthew 1:18-19; 2:13-18). Satan often begins his attack on God's sanctified children upon conception. Consider the number of miscarriages, abortions, premature babies, and childhood illnesses that occur on an annual basis (the Devil doesn't cause all these, but he does cause some, and he rejoices in all of them).

I do not know how Satan identifies God's potential for each

human life. What I can consider is my own being and the blows he deliberately landed throughout my life in an attempt to destroy my faith.

After discovering that she was pregnant with me, my mother began to have severe abdominal pain and was rushed to the hospital. She was told by the doctor that I was a tubal pregnancy and that she would require surgery to dispose of the embryo (me) in order to save her own life. She agreed to do so, but God had different plans, intervening in a way that only he could. He knew the plans that he had for me, plans for good and not for evil, a plan to prosper my growth, not hinder it (see Jeremiah 29:11). Miraculously, when the doctor performed the surgery, he discovered that I had moved from the fallopian tubes into my mother's uterus without any problems. I was born eight months later.

Satan was not pleased with my survival. He had tried unsuccessfully to take me out of the picture. Therefore, shortly after I was born he came into my life through the evil desires of others who stole my innocence through all types of abuse. I was sexually violated by two family members and a neighbor, and my father was physically, emotionally, and verbally abusive to me. To further complicate the issue, my family was steeped in various aspects of the occult. Because I didn't have the reasoning skills to challenge such an upbringing, I fell headfirst into a variety of high-risk behaviors and blatant sin in every area of my life. But God is faithful. He had other plans for me.

I gave my heart to Jesus Christ as my Savior when I was twenty-four years old. At that time I would have laughed at the possibility that God could use a wounded child such as myself to teach others, but he has done so, exceeding anything I've ever imagined for myself or others. Due to the viciousness of the attacks against my life and the fact that I teach about spiritual warfare—sharing God's tools to set believers free from the bondage of the enemy—I can't help but wonder if the Devil realized—a long time ago—that I have a special calling and that he needed to destroy this growing seed before it bloomed.

The good news is that God's plans are bigger and better, more powerful and resilient than any assault the enemy may make on the life of any child. My parents did not turn to God on my behalf to advocate and intercede for my life; so my Heavenly Father faithfully stepped into that role. He will do the same in your child's life, but he does not want to do this apart from human servants. First and foremost, it is our role, right, and responsibility as parents to teach, empower, and wage war on behalf of our children. Parents, allow me to share one of the most profound statements in the Bible to sound the trumpet in your heart regarding this topic. When Esther's people were facing imminent destruction, "ethnic cleansing," Mordecai told her:

> *Do not think to yourself that in the king's palace you will escape any more than all the other Jews. For if you keep silent at this time, relief and deliverance will rise for the Jews from another place, but you and your father's house will perish. And who knows whether you have not come to the kingdom for such a time as this?*
>
> ESTHER 4:13-14

Think of it—it wasn't enough for Esther to believe that God would protect his earthly people—she had to act on their behalf. In the same way, it is not enough for us to believe that God will watch over our children—we must act on their behalf, in faith, trusting the Lord to use our actions to protect our sons and daughters and to bring them into a full relationship with him!

THE FORTITUDE
OF MARRIAGE

Every marriage begins with the union of two incompatible
people in an impossible relationship. The task God gives us
in marriage is to turn it into something beautiful. With
God's grace—it can be done.

DR. ARCHIBALD HART,
HEALING LIFE'S HIDDEN ADDICTIONS

Parenting is the hardest job I've ever had. As exhilarating and rewarding as it is at most times, it can also be challenging, demanding, and
heart-wrenching. Our Creator knows firsthand how difficult being a
parent can be, for he too experiences the pleasure and heartache that
it entails. The fact that parenting is challenging is one reason why, in
his original plan, it was ordained to be done as a partnership between
a man and a woman. The irony behind this union is that two people
who join together in marriage to create one flesh are stronger than
both individuals apart from one another (Ecclesiastes 4:9-12).

God said that his intention from the beginning was that marriage
would be a picture of the relationship between Christ and his church
(Ephesians 5:22-25, 32). Because of this, Satan does anything possible to interfere with the blessing of marriage, aiming at leaving life-

long damage to both parties and the fruit of their loins—children. Statistics reveal that he is meeting his goal. *Each year* over one million American children suffer the divorce of their parents, and between six and fourteen million children are living with a gay or lesbian parent.[12] These statistics can incapacitate a believing child's awareness of who he or she is in Christ.

As a single parent for most of my children's lives, I can see firsthand the debilitating effects of divorce on their maturity, coping and social skills, survival mechanisms, and identity in Christ. Research regarding the effects of divorce on children support my own personal experience.

• Children whose parents have divorced are increasingly the victims of abuse. They exhibit more health, behavioral, and emotional problems, are involved more frequently in crime and drug abuse, and have higher rates of suicide.

• Children of divorced parents perform more poorly in reading, spelling, and math. They are more likely to repeat a grade and to have higher dropout rates and lower rates of college graduation.

• Families with children that were not poor before the divorce see their income drop as much as 50 percent. Almost 50 percent of the parents with children who are going through a divorce move into poverty after the divorce.

• Religious worship, which has been linked to better health, longer marriages, and better family life, declines after the parents' divorce.

Mothers are almost eight times more likely than fathers to be custodial parents.[13] As a result, children from fatherless homes account for:

• 63 percent of youth suicides.[14]
• 71 percent of pregnant teenagers.[15]
• 90 percent of all homeless and runaway children.[16]
• 70 percent of juveniles in state-operated institutions.[17]
• 85 percent of all children who exhibit behavioral disorders.[18]
• 80 percent of rapists motivated with displaced anger.[19]
• 71 percent of all high-school dropouts.[20]
• 75 percent of all adolescent patients in chemical abuse centers.[21]

- 85 percent of all youths in prisons.[22]
- "Three out of four teenage suicides occur in households where a parent has been absent."[23]
- "Fatherless children are at dramatically greater risk of suicide."[24]
- "In a study of 146 adolescent friends of 26 adolescent suicide victims, teens living in single-parent families are not only more likely to commit suicide, but also more likely to suffer from psychological disorders, when compared to teens living in intact families."[25]

These statistics are not meant to bombard the single parent with blame, shame, or guilt. On the contrary, I share them to show you how vulnerable our children are to the dangers of the world's influence, their flesh, and satanic assault when the spiritual covering of the marital union is shattered. God wants us to be aware of Satan's schemes and to guard against them (2 Corinthians 2:11; Ephesians 6:11).

Excluding an abusive environment, research does not show that it is more or less destructive for a child to live with a male or female single parent. What is revealed, however, is that children raised in a two-parent home are more likely to succeed and grow into healthier adults. That's not to say that a single parent cannot raise a healthy child. In fact, God is the Father to the fatherless (Psalm 68:5). He knew that due to our fallen nature, he would have to step up to the plate in his children's lives, and he promises to defend the cause of the fatherless (Deuteronomy 10:18). Thus we can expect him to rise above any and all statistics and research and to meet the needs of our children when we petition him to do so and as our children allow him access to the pain and rejection resulting from an absent parent.

I will discuss more about the specific strategy for single parents (and those in unequally yoked marriages) in regard to spiritual warfare in the next chapter. For now, however, let's look at the power and responsibility of warfare for the believing couple.

THE POWER OF PARENTAL UNITY

There is power in numbers. As a matter of fact, Ecclesiastes 4:9-12 affirms to us that the marital union interwoven with God is powerful:

Two are better than one, because they have a good reward for their toil. For if they fall, one will lift up his fellow. But woe to him who is alone when he falls and has not another to lift him up! Again, if two lie together, they keep warm, but how can one keep warm alone? And though a man might prevail against one who is alone, two will withstand him—a threefold cord is not quickly broken.

Few passages in the Bible are as profound as this one when it comes to the strength found in the marital union of two who turn to Jesus Christ in their marriage. There are times in every marriage when one part of the union is weaker or stronger than the other, and as the saying goes, "You are only as strong as your weakest link." In a spiritually sound marriage, each partner is continually lifting the other up through prayer, encouragement, and God's promises. Some say that sex is the thermometer that measures the health of the rest of the marriage, but I disagree. Spiritual intimacy between two individuals is essential to the welfare of a marriage, exposing both its cancerous areas and its healthy parts.

SATAN'S METHODS FOR DESTROYING MARRIAGES

When a single, Christian adult meets a like-minded individual, and marriage looks imminent, all kinds of assumptions and expectations fill both their heads. One is, *No matter what we go through, we will be able to overcome it. We are believers. Through Christ we can deal with anything.* This goal is honorable, biblically based, and 100 percent correct. But sadly, in many Christian marriages when the proverbial rubber hits the road, conflict arises, and the same two people are soon sitting on opposite sides of a conference table, letting two lawyers decide the fate of their future and their children. How does this happen?

Let's explore the reality of such a situation for a moment in relation to an all-consuming physical illness—cancer. Our Creator designed our bodies to be a collection of millions of different types of cells. Normally cells grow and divide to produce more cells when the body needs them. This orderly process helps keep the body healthy. In a spiritually sound marriage, a similar process takes place.

Although the marital union is made up of two individuals, they are one, working together as a team in the Body of Christ to produce healthy cells—fruit of the Spirit that is a reflection of Christ in them as a couple, which in turn is handed down to their children. These "children" may or may not be biological. They may also be individuals we've been called to disciple, take under our wings to mentor, or counsel. Whether or not their DNA is connected to ours, they are part of us because they are part of the Body of Christ.

But sometimes cells in the physical body keep dividing when new cells are not needed. These cells may form a mass of extra tissue called a growth or tumor. Tumors can be benign or malignant. Benign tumors are not cancerous. They can usually be removed, and in most cases they don't come back. The most important point regarding benign tumors is that this type of growth does not invade other tissues and does not spread to other parts of the body. Benign tumors are not a threat to life in most cases. I liken benign tumors to a complacent marriage, one that just seems to go through life on autopilot, never really experiencing spiritual growth or love with depth. Such a marriage, like a benign tumor, is not a threat to the enemy, nor does it spread to other parts of the Body of Christ, including the couple's children.

The problem with this marriage is that it is subject, like the couple's children, to falling away from what they may initially have known to be true in Christ. As a result, as mentioned in Matthew 13:3-6, they fall "along the path" or "on rocky ground":

> *A sower went out to sow. And as he sowed, some seeds fell along the path, and the birds came and devoured them. Other seeds fell on rocky ground, where they did not have much soil, and immediately they sprang up, since they had no depth of soil, but when the sun rose they were scorched. And since they had no root, they withered away.*

There are a lot of reasons why persons may not take root in the faith of Jesus Christ. To examine several of them would require another book, but we will explore a couple in regard to the family.

One essential reason is because their own parents' faith was mediocre at best. Another is because they have what I call an "inherited faith"; that is, they have a strong family heritage in Christ and basically believe they will slide into heaven on their forefathers' and foremothers' coattails. Regardless of the reason, while an initial confession of faith in Christ was made at some point in their lives, these halfhearted believers generally do not mature in their newfound faith and thus do not make an impact on the rest of the body or on unsaved individuals. Eventually they remove themselves from Christian fellowship or are "cut . . . down" by the Master Vinedresser, as described in Luke 13:6-7:

> A man had a fig tree planted in his vineyard, and he came seeking fruit on it and found none. And he said to the vinedresser, "Look, for three years now I have come seeking fruit on this fig tree, and I find none. Cut it down. Why should it use up the ground?"

Malignant tumors are cancerous and can be compared to an unhealthy marriage. Cells in these tumors can invade and damage nearby tissues and organs. It's important to note here, specifically in correlation to the marital union, that every type of cancer originally manifests from microscopic cells that cannot be seen by the human eye. Few people have gone into the marital union with the goal of divorce, but statistics reveal that approximately half of them will divorce. What brings two people who are committed to God and one another to dissolve the union completely? In many cases tiny offenses have planted themselves in the fertilized soil of a heart that without the love, forgiveness, and patience of Jesus Christ is deceptive above all things, and soon this turns into a full-fledged malignant cancer that overcomes the union and results in a marital break. Like malignant tumors in the body, divorce invades *every* relationship within the scope of that union and damages them, especially the children.

Whenever two different people from two different backgrounds with various childhood issues come together, there are going to be problems. Equally so, whenever you take two people who come from similar backgrounds who have no childhood issues (which I have never seen) but have a sin nature (which we all have), there are going to be problems! How rapidly and how effectively we work through such issues will determine the spiritual health of our marriage. I love Ephesians 4:26-27, a foundational Scripture for every marriage, because every marriage will inevitably encounter spiritual warfare: "Do not let the sun go down while you are still angry, and do not give the devil a foothold" (NIV).

Couples absolutely cannot afford *not* to discuss infractions, offenses, and disappointments in their spouse with their spouse. To do so is to allow a foothold for the enemy, and to allow him access into their marriage is to allow cancerous cells to run amok. In the physical body, malignant cancer cells run rampant without medical intervention, and so do unresolved issues in marriage apart from the healing of Jesus Christ. Sometimes the Lord uses Christian counselors, pastors, and others to be his hands to help put the balm of Gilead on wounds in a dying marriage. Do not be embarrassed or timid about asking for the Great Physician's help.

You may wonder why, in a spiritual warfare book for parents, I'm discussing the spiritual health of your marriage. I do so because of Mark 3:25: "If a house is divided against itself, that house will not be able to stand." If there is not unity in your marriage, Satan will relentlessly attack your marital union. Satan's war tactics are subtle but methodical. Like many historical military commanders in the past, Satan's main objective is to disrupt communication and to create a mutiny among the leadership. If he can succeed in doing so, he wins the war at hand—and perhaps for generations to come. It's important to note that the immune system in a healthy body is continually fighting and overcoming cancerous cells that are attacking the body. It's when the immune system is functioning at less than its capacity that it falls behind and the unhealthy illness begins to overtake the body.

A normal, healthy marriage is similar. Individually and as a couple, you must continually fight the world, the enemy, and your own sin nature in order not to take offense with your mate. Perhaps you do pretty well most of the time, but when you're tired, have had a long day, are dealing with an excessive amount of stress, or whatever, those offenses build up, one on another. Pretty soon they will begin to consume your marriage, and that man or woman at the office who listens to you and seems lighthearted and carefree starts looking pretty good. Or maybe it gets easier for you to complain about your mate to your friends, which only intensifies your offense against your partner. Do you see how this can snowball? Eventually you stop talking to your partner and start talking to someone else. That's a major red flag that needs immediate attention, including going to your partner and discussing the microscopic offense that initially started the process of pain in the first place.

The most effective way a couple can have spiritual unity is through the very avenue that the enemy of our soul attempts to destroy: communication—that is, honestly conversing first and foremost together with God and, secondly, with one another. When I hear couples tell me they don't have time to talk, pray, or read the Bible together, I tell them they can't afford *not* to make time. The bottom line is, we make time for the things that are important to us. If your priorities are in proper order, you'll make communication with God and your mate, as well as biblical devotions, a vital part of your daily life.

The majority of conflict in marriage stems from miscommunication or a lack of communication on a variety of issues. In Ephesians 4:1-3 the apostle Paul urges those in the Body of Christ to live a life worthy of the calling they have received by living together in love and unity. This cannot be done without conversing with one another and together before God. If I could stress one point to couples, it would be that Satan desires to destroy your marriage. He will tempt you to become offended at your mate over simple things, will fill your schedules with unnecessary things to do so you don't have time to talk and pray, will create havoc through other people, and will even at times use your children to create a wedge between the two of you.

Consider for a moment you and your mate's weakest areas. Are you prone to overwork? Do you have difficulty saying no to the requests of others? Do you put your children above your mate? Do you have a tendency to gossip or slander? Are you overly sensitive to rejection due to childhood wounds? Have you had an addiction in your past? Whatever you or your mate's Achilles' heel is, you can be sure that's exactly where the enemy is aiming a fiery dart. Satan doesn't play fair. He has no sympathy, compassion, or empathy for God's children. He is relentless and will do whatever it takes to destroy any representation or reflection of Jesus Christ and his descendants.

Another crucial area in which we lose biblical vision is that of team or partnership mentality. When our mate offends us and we do not work our way through the steps of forgiveness efficiently, we can begin to see our partner as an enemy. Husbands and wives are a team, coworkers on the same side of the spiritual battle. Even when our mates sin by saying or doing something offensive, that does not justify an attitude that regards them as our spiritual enemy. What we need is a new, forgiving perspective.

A NEW PERSPECTIVE ON FORGIVENESS

There was a season in my walk with Christ when I was struggling to forgive myself for things that I had done as a believer, as well as forgiving things that had been done to me by someone I had been involved with. One day as I sat with my friend and Christian counselor Cindy Fitzee, she showed me a picture of Jesus carrying the cross. She said, "Leslie, when you hold yourself to the sins of the past, you are saying that what Jesus did on the cross wasn't enough. In essence, you're saying that you have to carry your own sin. But you're not the savior of your own life."

It was like she had tossed a lit match into my soul. Long after I left her office, her words resonated in my spirit. I realized she was right. I needed to ask forgiveness from God for trying to carry my own sinful past. What Christ did for me on Calvary was sufficient for all my sins—past, present, and future.

After I prayed for forgiveness, the Lord showed me that I was doing the same thing with the other believer who had harmed me. If what Christ did on the cross was enough for my sin, it was also enough for his sin. If what Jesus did on Calvary could change my life and behavior, it had the power to do the same in his life. Who was I to hold back forgiveness in the relationship? Who was I to be bitter over past offenses?

I fell to my knees again, this time asking forgiveness for acting as if Christ's finished work on the cross wasn't enough for the person who had harmed me. Once I prayed that prayer, I was able to view this person in a whole new light—through the eyes of Jesus.

Another tool I've used with myself I call *recollecting offenses*. What generally happens in my life is that someone hurts me, and I take that offense and nurture it, bathe in self-pity, and build a mountain of reasons why I should not forgive that individual. Let me give you an example. Suppose someone lies to me. Don't you just hate it when someone leads you astray with a falsehood? I can really get on a soapbox about that one! But when I stop and recollect all the times I've lied to people, I'm suddenly humbled by my own sin. I may have had what I thought was a good reason to lie to someone, but the person who lied to me may have felt the same way. In both cases it's wrong. Nevertheless, I have more empathy and understanding toward the person who lied to me when I consider that I am not above the same sin. My heart is thus humbled, and I offer forgiveness more readily.

When we hold onto unforgiveness, a level of self-righteousness and self-exaltation accompanies our attitude. But when we take the time to look at the reality and honesty of how we've treated other people, we see ourselves equal to them—sinners in need of God's grace, forgiveness, and restoration.

THE FREEDOM OF FORGIVENESS

Christians make forgiveness much more difficult than it has to be. We want to punish ourselves and others for sins that have been committed. We mistakenly believe that if we forgive someone, we are saying that what that person did was OK. Not so. Furthermore, forgiveness is not an invitation for another person to hurt us again; neither does it mean that we will immediately trust that person again.

Forgiveness simply means that we give up our right to hold onto the wrongdoings of others against us. We release them from their debt to us, accepting the consequence of their actions against us. That's what Christ did. He released us from our debt and accepted a horrific death on our behalf. The truth is that holding a grudge or holding others in debt ensnares *us*, not *them*. Accepting the consequences of their actions against us is often simply an issue of perspective. In most cases we are already living with the consequences of the other person's actions. The person who harmed us has usually gone on with his or her life, unaware of the pain that he or she has inflicted on us. The most difficult spiritual battles that we face in marriage will be issues of forgiveness. And many of the strongholds with which we struggle—bitterness, hatred, jealousy, gossip, slander—are direct results of unforgiveness.

The way to work through the spiritual battle of unforgiveness that rages within us is to keep taking it to the cross and to keep giving it over to Jesus. There is a process that I recommend to believers that enables them to break the bonds a besetting sin—a sin to which they return time and again. I call this process "the Five Rs." I want to apply it here to this issue of unforgiveness:

- *Recognize* that you are refusing to forgive.
- *Renounce* your sin of unforgiveness.
- *Rebuke* the spirit of unforgiveness that you've nurtured.
- *Receive* truth in its place.
- *Rejoice* in the freedom that you now have in Christ.

Learn and practice these five Rs, and you will discover that forgiveness doesn't make you a victim. It allows you to walk with Jesus victoriously.

THE CONFUSION OF OUR BIBLICAL JOB DESCRIPTIONS

One of the most prominent problems in marriages today is the confusion centered around the biblical roles of husband and wife. Women find the topic of submission distasteful because it's been lorded over them and society has distorted the biblical definition. In conjunction, many men have either stepped down from their role as spiritual leaders or have become tyrants in the home in an attempt to bring order and control. Many homes have become breeding beds for rebellion and hatred. It is vital that we understand the importance of both roles and the attack against marriages in these ways or we will see more and more marriages fail.

Let's consider a brief biblical history of leadership, submission, and servanthood.

We all know the story of Adam and Eve in the Garden of Eden. God created the world, including the Garden of Eden, and he created Adam, placing him in the garden to care for it. It was a paradise, complete with its own river and trees that were pleasing to the eye. God told Adam that he could eat from any tree in the garden except from the tree of the knowledge of good and evil. To eat from that tree would result in death.

Then God said, "It is not good for the man to be alone. I will make a helper suitable for him" (Genesis 2:18, NIV). And he did. God caused Adam to fall into a deep slumber, and, taking one of Adam's ribs, he created Eve. When Adam awoke and saw Eve he said, "Wow! Holy Moley!" or something like that. Okay, he actually said, "This at last is bone of my bones and flesh of my flesh; she shall be called Woman, because she was taken out of Man" (2:23).

Adam and Eve lived in the garden until the serpent, who was craftier than any of the wild animals that God had made, entered the scene. And where did the serpent—the Devil—head? Where he always goes. He went for the weakest link—something he will always do in our marriages. Now, sister, before you write me a letter telling me you're *not* weaker than your husband, let me remind you of God's Word in 1 Peter 3:7: "husbands, live with your wives in an understanding way, showing honor to the woman as the weaker vessel, since they are heirs with you of the grace of life, so that your prayers may not be hindered."

Weaker than our male counterparts—that is the way God designed us. He did that to help us fulfill his commandment to submit to our husbands. It is when we are weak that we seek help. Women are prone to do it all without the help of others. Consider everything you do on a day-to-day basis—wash dishes, do laundry, run errands, discipline the children, buy groceries or clothes, and more. Some of you even work full-time outside of your household duties. It seems only natural to do it all by yourself, but that was not God's plan. He doesn't want us to be female Lone Rangers. He wants us to work as a team with our mate, under the headship of our

Captain, Jesus Christ. Because of the way God ordained and created the marital union, Satan went to Eve instead of to Adam. And he did so for a specific reason.

THE NECK THAT TURNS THE HEAD

You've probably heard the saying, "The man may be the head of the family, but the woman is the neck that turns the head." Satan knew he could get to the man by deceiving the woman. Satan's deception of Eve began with planting a seed of doubt. There was no courteous exchange with the serpent. No "Hey, nice day in paradise, isn't it? How are you today?" Satan's first recorded words were, "Did God *really* say, 'You must not eat from any tree in the garden'?" (3:1, NIV, emphasis added). Consider your own marriage. What has Satan whispered in your ear? What has created doubt with regard to what God has said about marriage?

I've heard many women apply that same satanic logic to their marriages.

• "Did God really say that I must stay married to my husband or that I must never remarry?"

• "Did God really say that I have to submit to my husband, even if I don't agree?"

• "Did God really say that the only reason I can divorce is because of adultery?"

Back to Eve. She responded by repeating the command that God had given Adam. "We may eat of the fruit of the trees in the garden, but God said, 'You shall not eat of the fruit of the tree that is in the midst of the garden, neither shall you touch it, lest you die'" (3:2-3). For the most part, Eve was simply repeating what God had said to Adam. In order for her to obey God's directive, she had to believe and trust *whom*? Her husband. And to do so, she had to be confident that he had advised her correctly.

Satan's response created doubt and was an obvious contradiction of God's instructions. He said, "You will *not* surely die" (3:4, emphasis added). The snake then slandered God, claiming that God was keeping something good from them: "God knows that when you eat of it your eyes will be opened, and you will be like God, knowing good and evil" (3:5).

Eve then made the wrong decision. She not only partook of the fruit, but she gave some to her husband, who was with her, and he ate it. But Adam's silence spoke volumes. He failed to restrain or redirect Eve. He failed as the spiritual leader. Ashamed and aware of their nakedness, Adam and Eve then hid. God entered the garden and began calling to the man. Adam explained to God that he now realized that he was naked. God asked if he had eaten of the forbidden tree. Adam basically responded by telling the truth, but he shifted the blame first to God for giving Eve to him, then to Eve. "The woman whom you gave to be with me, she gave me fruit of the tree, and I ate" (3:12). Then God said to Eve, "What is this that you have done?" (3:13). So Eve blamed the snake: "The serpent deceived me, and I ate" (3:13). It is true that the snake deceived Eve, but she *chose* to disobey God by believing the lie of the serpent, and Adam *chose* to follow his wife down the road of disobedience and not stand up for what he knew was right in God's eyes.

God cursed the snake first, saying, "Because you have done this, cursed are you above all livestock and above all beasts of the field; on your belly you shall go, and dust you shall eat all the days of your life" (3:14). Then comes an important conclusion to the curse on the snake. God said in verse 15, "I will put enmity between you and the woman, and between your offspring and her offspring; he shall bruise your head, and you shall bruise his heel." Notice that God first said that there would be enmity—hostility—between Satan and the woman. But in relation to spiritual warfare for parents, the verse tells us that there will be enmity between the Devil's offspring (that is, his children) and the woman's (our children). Do you see the biblical grounds for believing there is a spiritual assault on our children?

A CURSE AND A PROMISE

The Hebrew word translated "enmity" is *'eybah*, meaning "hatred, hostility; to be an enemy." Satan is your enemy, and you are his. God gave women extraordinary power through persuasion, beauty, gentleness, and servanthood. Satan knows that if the same persuasive skill he used to lead Adam astray is used for God's glory, he's in bad shape. That is why he is determined to destroy woman and her godly characteristics; if he can do so, he crushes man as well. And if he crushes man, he crushes the world. We do not have to look far in Scripture to see examples of this. Consider Solomon's wives who led him astray and into worshiping foreign gods, or Delilah and her seduction of Samson, or Jezebel who walked all over her husband and led his kingdom to ruin.

After cursing the snake, God addressed Eve: "I will surely multiply your pain in childbearing; in pain you shall bring forth children. Your desire shall be for your husband, and he shall rule over you" (3:16). In those moments of greatest blessing—marriage and the birth of children—the woman would sense most clearly the painful consequences of her rebellion against God. Thankfully, along with this discouraging pronouncement there is also a promise: the final victory will belong to the seed of the woman. In the birth of every child, therefore, there is a reminder of the hope that lay in God's promise. Birth pains are not merely a reminder of the futility of the fall—they are a sign of impending joy as well.

The second part of verse 16 is vital for us to grasp: "Your desire shall be for your husband, and he shall rule over you." The word "desire" means "to yearn or long for something that is not yours to possess." As a result, a woman's tendency is to resist her husband's leadership, regarding it as something that *she* should have. We don't have to look far in history to see the fulfillment of this judgment. Ever since the Fall woman has been resisting man's leadership, and that is one of the central problems in marriages today. This has nothing to do with the essential equality of men and women. It is simply a question of the God-given *roles* of men and women and the tendency of women to usurp a man's role. This is an issue that women need to address honestly in the Body of Christ. And whenever we violate God's plan, we need to repent.

Equally so, the man has a responsibility to lead his wife and children according to God's principles. Historically, many men have gravitated to one end of the spectrum or the other; they are dominant and spiritually abusive or passive and spiritually inactive. Both behaviors are sinful.

When Scripture says, "Your desire shall be for your husband, and he shall rule over you," the word "rule" means "to govern, have dominion, and manage." The natural and sinful tendency is for the man to take this to the extreme and oppress or dictate, or to submit— that is, to give way and let his wife rule the roost. Apart from the Holy Spirit, by whom alone we can find balance, man can waver either way.

RECAPTURING OUR BIBLICAL ROLES

No matter how noble and fulfilling a woman's career outside the home may be, it is not an acceptable endeavor when it takes place at the expense of marriages and children. Furthermore, no matter how skilled your wife is with leading your home or being a spiritual leader, that is not a role God has ultimately given to her. If you are not a part of a partnership that exists on more than paper, you are not in a biblical marriage. God intended for marriages to last until "death do us part," for children to be raised by both parents, and for the man to be the spiritual leader. Many families could do without some extras and live on one income in order to have the mother focus primarily on raising her children and investing in her marriage. The world's way screams for us to "keep up with the Joneses," for women to manifest certain aspects of masculinity, and for men to sit back and let their wives run their lives. But what our world truly needs is for couples to choose God's way instead of the world's way.

The ultimate role of both the husband and the wife is to reflect the image of Jesus to the other in all each says and does. It is the godly woman's role, responsibility, and privilege to minister to her husband. Equally so, it is the godly husband's role, responsibility, and privilege to love his wife as Christ loves the church.

It is the responsibility of each of us to seek God's wisdom through his Word, comparing our core beliefs about marriage to his truth. We must examine the world's concept of marriage in light of *God's* plan for marriage. These are the areas where we need to petition God for his help in order to learn and apply his truth in our marriages. Don't be misled. This is a spiritual battle in which Satan will not easily give up. He knows that if we walk in rebellion or independence from our mates, we will surely experience broken fellowship with God and spiritual ruin. Satan will then succeed in his destruction of the family unit, which will certainly sabotage our children and their grandchildren for generations to come.

In Civil War literature "defeat in detail" means to defeat a force unit by unit, usually because the individual regiments or companies are not within supporting distance of one another. This is exactly what happens in a marriage when the wife continually usurps the authority of her husband, and the man allows it to happen. Looking back on the season when my children still lived at home and I was married, I can recall several examples of this. My husband would withhold permission for the children to participate in some activity, and I would undermine him by later allowing them to do what he had denied them permission to do. Or I would say things that subtly degraded him, like, "Well, you know how your father is; he's never really handled things like that well." Such situations may seem minor, but they teach our children that their father's authority is not valid, that they don't have to respect it. This "defeat in detail" frequently occurs in families where one parent does not support the other. Therein lies one more reason why children of divorce struggle so severely: the united front that God created for them in parents is missing.

When we submit to our husband's authority, we do so as unto God first and our husband second. When we usurp our husband's authority, we are telling God, and our husband, that we aren't going to listen. When husbands allow their wives to be the leaders, they are being lazy and sinful. Our calling is to submit to the roles that God has given to us as husbands and wives.

BIBLICAL LEADERSHIP AND SUBMISSION

Are we always to submit, in every circumstance? Is it ever right *not* to submit? In Colossians 3:18 wives are told, "submit to your husbands, as is fitting in the Lord."

What does "fitting in the Lord" mean? The meaning of the word *submit* is "to place in an orderly fashion, to place under." That does not mean that we mindlessly obey our husbands if they command us to do something that violates clear biblical teaching. We must, instead, weigh submission to our husbands against the Word of God, making it fitting in the Lord.

If we are living our lives in submission to God, submission to our husbands will naturally occur. The only circumstance in which you should *not* submit would be if your husband requests you to do something that is against God's Word. I knew a woman who said that she started watching pornographic movies with her husband because he said she had to submit to him and that's what he wanted her to do. I knew another woman who endured years of physical abuse under the guise of submission. Both of these examples are *not* in submission to God because they are contrary to his Word. They are abusive distortions of God's Word, done for self-satisfaction.

When we submit to the biblically based leadership of our husbands, we are following the plan for womanhood that God designed at the beginning of creation. If we are married, that means that we ought to submit to the authority of our husbands as God intended. The danger against which we must guard is the tendency to seek to overthrow that authority, causing havoc in our marriages, our families, and ultimately our nation.

On the other side of the coin, it is the husband's responsibility to love his wife with the passion, respect, honor, and sacrifice that Jesus demonstrated on behalf of all believers. Further, the godly husband must delve into God's Word and actively find and mirror this role for his wife and children. His wife's submission should not be under his control. Loving her as Christ loves the church is not past tense, nor should it focus on current offenses, but instead it should be sacrificial love for all behavior.

4

THE SINGLE PARENT

All your children shall be taught by the LORD,
and great shall be the peace of your children.

ISAIAH 54:13

My children are raised now, and I have been blessed with two beautiful grandsons. But for most of my children's lives I was not married. Looking back, I can see both the pros and cons to this circumstance. On one hand, my relationship with the Lord became more intimate because I was forced to cling to him as my Husband in every way. When my children rebelled I went to *him* for guidance and wisdom. When money was short and the kids had to have a physical for a sporting event, or when an unexpected expense presented itself that I hadn't budgeted for, I went to *him* for provision. When I was exhausted from working full-time outside the home and came home to another full-time job cooking, cleaning, and being the proverbial taxi, I went to *him* for renewed strength. He *never* failed me, *always* providing the necessities for me and my children as I clung to him. I *never* felt abandoned or alone.

On the other hand, at times I was lonely. I desired to have a Christian mate to talk to, someone who could encourage me in the

Lord if I wanted to give up when the battle was the fiercest. Someone who would not be afraid to go on the front line of the battle on behalf of our children, someone to remind me that there would come a time when all parental heartache would disappear and we'd spend eternity without pain, worry, and anxiety.

As a leader in the workforce who had to make numerous vital decisions on a day-to-day basis and who had to be strong in the most horrendous circumstances, I wanted someone in my home I could be weak around. I wanted a spiritual covering that would shelter me from the torrid rains of the world and the brutal attacks of the enemy. These are all natural, God-given desires. God was faithful to me during these lonely moments, always comforting me, assuring me that eventually that time would come. In the meantime he provided (and continues to provide) other believers to meet various needs for me and my children.

I was a women's leader in my church. So I was often the one others came to for advice, but in his graciousness, the Lord provided older, godly women to come alongside me and direct me in child-rearing, single parenthood, and maturity in Christ. Additionally, as a single-parent I made sure I was on the top of the prayer list at my church. I would even go online to various Internet sites that took prayer requests and asked others to pray about specific issues I was struggling with in regard to my children. Eventually as I met single brothers in the Lord who were looking for ways to help, I would ask them to specifically pray for my children, mentor them when necessary as a "spiritual father," and occasionally call in the evenings and touch base with my kids. To this day my children still stay in contact with some of those people, who have since married and had children of their own. I met a lot of godly, single men who became good friends. Sometimes they would call and read the Word of God to me and pray with me; then we would discuss what was read. They did not fill the intimate needs of a husband, nor were they potential mates, but they were able to provide male friendship, laughter, and biblical guidance and wisdom during those times.

The Body of Christ was designed to work together toward one purpose, just as the human body is designed to function in unity to provide life. Single mothers can help single fathers and vice versa when the need becomes evident. I would strongly caution single parents against involving the opposite sex in their child's life if the other person is married, unless the couple will minister to you or your child as a team.

If you are married and your mate is an unbeliever and non-supportive, you are in a very difficult and different circumstance, but not a hopeless one. While we were no longer married, when I became a believer, my children's father mocked my faith in Christ, undermined my parental skills, and was almost nonexistent in the childrearing process. That made for a tough battle when decisions had to be made together for the benefit of the children. Being married to an unbeliever can be similar. He may not understand why you prefer to send your child to a Christian school instead of a secular one. He may think it foolish to spend time praying or interceding on your child's behalf. He is not able to wash you in the Word, spiritually encourage you when you are down, or hold your arms up in battle. In many ways you may feel like a single parent.

Find like-minded women in your church to pray for and with you. If possible, meet with another woman one-on-one once a week who will "sponsor" you and your children. Take part of your time together to discuss specific issues you are grappling with, then take the rest of the time to pray together. If your mate is not a believer but is supportive of your faith and your desire to raise your children for God, perhaps he will allow another person or couple to step in and "spiritually adopt" your child to help you. All of these decisions need to be prayed over and discussed with your mate. There are great lessons to be learned from the book of Esther about dealing with an unsaved mate, such as waiting on God's timing, the spiritual fruit of prayer, and trusting in the Lord.

For both the single parent and the person who is married to an unbeliever, I want to emphasize one point that helped me tremendously during my single years: whether you're a male or a female, cling to God as though he is your spouse. I could tell you story after story about how the Lord has become real to me as my Husband, but to close this chapter I'll share just one.

My engine failed on my truck right after my warranty expired. As a single parent I was on a really strict budget and did not have the eight-hundred-plus dollars needed to fix the vehicle. It was the only vehicle I had. To make matters worse, the alarm system malfunctioned and went off whenever the vehicle wasn't running, and it couldn't be disconnected without the necessary repairs. It was a hopeless situation to the human eye. I had no other choice but to have the dealership fix it, but I knew I didn't have the money.

For three hours I sat in the dealership waiting room praying for a miracle. I told the Lord, "You say you are my Husband, and I believe that to be true. As my Husband you see the situation I am in and know that I don't have the money to pay for these repairs. I don't know how you are going to provide, but I trust that you will." For every one of those three hours I stood on various promises found in the Bible. I refused to let doubt creep in and steal the promises to which I was clinging. After my truck was fixed, the maintenance manager pulled me aside and asked me to talk with him one on one. He said, "We don't usually do this, but we aren't going to charge you for fixing your truck." I wept in joy—my Husband had intervened on my behalf! The point of this story is to cling to him. Cling to him more than you ever have to anyone, but like you've always dreamt of doing with a godly mate, remembering that God is a rewarder of those who earnestly seek him (Hebrews 11:6).

When your wife or husband doesn't know the Lord as his or her Savior, you have extra prayer duty—for your children and for your mate. Specific ways to pray for your mate may include asking the Lord to drop the scales of deception from his or her eyes so that he or she will see truth; that as a deer pants for water, his or her soul will desire him; that your mate will see Jesus and the blessings of following him in your daily walk; that the Lord will soften his or her heart to hear how he has changed your life.

Additionally, you can intercede in the spirit realm and bind all evil spirits that are hindering your mate from hearing or seeing the truth, so that any and all of Satan's weapons to keep your mate from hearing the truth of the gospel will be extinguished, and so the Devil will release all traps in the name of Jesus that are keeping him or her bound to falsehood (2 Timothy 2:25-26; Acts 26:18).

One promise you have as a believer married to an unbeliever is found in Ephesians 1:4-6:

> *For he chose us in him before the creation of the world to be holy and blameless in his sight. In love he predestined us to be adopted as his sons through Jesus Christ, in accordance with his pleasure and will—to the praise of his glorious grace, which he has freely given us in the One he loves.* (NIV)

Several years ago I bought the books *Praying God's Will for My Daughter* and *Praying God's Will for My Son* by Lee Roberts. Both books have proved to be wonderful resources not only telling me *how* to pray for my children but *what* to pray. Every day, year after year, I'd pray for specific areas for my son and daughter that they were struggling with at that time. Between some of the topics Lee outlines in the books, there are blank pages on which I wrote notes to my children about what they were struggling with and how I was intervening for them in the spirit realm. As I've looked back over these books time and time again, I can clearly see where and how the Lord intervened in my children's lives and the growth and faith this developed in my relationship with him. I encourage all parents to find a resource such as Lee Roberts's books to help guide them when necessary.

THE SPIRITUAL COURTSHIP
OF OUR CHILDREN

*Again, the devil took him to a very high mountain and
showed him all the kingdoms of the world and their glory.
And he said to him, "All these I will give you, if you will
fall down and worship me."*

MATTHEW 4:8-9

Satan first attacked Jesus immediately after his conception by the
Holy Spirit in the womb of his mother, the virgin Mary, and we can
expect no less for our own children. Satan attacks all newborn children in some way, but he especially attacked Jesus because he is our
Messiah. Matthew 1:18 records that Mary was pledged to be married
to Joseph, but before they came together as husband and wife she was
found to be with child through the Holy Spirit. Because Joseph was a
righteous man and did not want to expose Mary to public disgrace,
he decided to divorce her quietly instead. Without God's intervention
and the pliable heart of Joseph, Mary would have been a single parent—an outcast in that day—raising our Savior. Satan often begins his
courtship, his attempt to lure the allegiance of human souls, by attacking God's sanctified children at conception. Consider the number of
miscarriages, abortions, premature, at-risk babies, and childhood ill-

nesses that occur on an annual basis. Of course, not all miscarriages and childhood illnesses are a result of attacks from Satan, but at the same time about 25 percent of the illnesses recorded in Scripture were caused by demons.

The next spiritual battle that Scripture records is shortly after Jesus' birth, when Herod sought to kill the Messiah. Numerous other assaults followed, from the Pharisees' jealous and arrogant actions to demons confronting Jesus when he performed miracles. There were attacks on him as he watched his friends and family experience life's heartaches and through the twelve disciples who deserted him in his greatest time of need. There was also his turmoil in the Garden of Gethsemane and his anguish on the cross. Even though Mel Gibson's movie *The Passion of the Christ* vividly portrays Jesus' physical anguish, there was no way it could adequately portray the spiritual battle as he defeated the Devil by bearing our sins and accomplishing our redemption. None of us will fully understand that aspect until we stand before our Maker.

THE ROOT OF SATANIC ATTACK

All of Satan's attacks stem from his desire to have power and control over God's creatures and creation. He is convinced that if he can attack us, God's children, in our most vulnerable places, we will turn away from God and accept the lie that following the Evil One is the better way. A clear example of this is his attempt to seduce Jesus in Matthew 4. The Devil offered Christ the world in exchange for his loyalty, his spiritual inheritance, and his faith. Jesus, of course, declined his offer. Satan offers us similar deals throughout our lives.

Many of his offers seem particularly attractive to our children. Why is that? Wealth and earthly treasure, success, and advancement represent power in today's society, and power leads to status. But all of this is temporary; in this world "moth and rust destroy and . . . thieves break in and steal" (Matthew 6:19). Proverbs 10:2 (NIV) describes such accomplishments as "ill-gotten treasures" with "no value." Yet we strive for them even to the point of treating others viciously in order to acquire them.

Satan knew he was speaking to the Son of God, the firstborn of all creation, so he fired with both barrels—a direct frontal assault against Jesus. With God's spiritual offspring, however, he is generally more subtle in his attacks. He deceives us into thinking that we are simply determined to gain the same worldly treasures that everyone else wants. In our striving, however, Satan leads us by a golden nose ring, escorting us down the shortcut to spiritual ruin. Let me give you a minor example that I ran across with my son, Paul, when he was about eight years old.

Paul came home from school one day with a round, cardboard-type toy called a pog. Pogs were used during that time similar to the way marbles were used forty years ago. The size, weight, and picture on the pog was similar in value to the clarity and color that a marble had. The goal of the game was to flip your opponent's pog upside down with a heavier game piece. If you were successful, you kept your opponent's pog as your own. For an eight-year-old, this was a big deal.

Pogs had different pictures on them, and each drawing or symbol had a specific value. A pog with an eight ball or skull on it was much more valuable than one with a flower or skateboard. My son became obsessed with winning and owning pogs with specific pictures on them because to own a specific pog represented power, success, and popularity. He became so enthralled with winning this game that he eventually began manipulating younger or more inexperienced children in order to get their pogs. This may seem like a minor example of the wealth and earthly treasures, success, and advancement pressures that we endure as adults. However, it is during a child's most pliable years of development (newborn to twelve years of age) that these unhealthy seeds are planted and fertilized through everyday interaction with others. Without intervention, these children grow up to be adults trying to "keep up with the Joneses."

Satan was deceiving my son (as he does us all) into believing that he was simply striving for the same worldly treasure that all the other kids wanted. In his striving, however, Satan was leading him down a road that would ultimately destroy him and his identity and purpose in life if there were no parental and heavenly intervention.

My daughter, Charlene, fell into a similar trap in her pre-teens. It involved her appearance. Charlene is vivacious and has never had a shortage of friends. The Lord designed her with an extra dose of personality and great communication skills, and he created her to be especially attractive. The combination of those gifts led to continual knocks on our door and a phone that rang endlessly as many boys courted her.

Somewhere around the age of thirteen, she began to grow unhealthily concerned with her appearance and the acceptance of other people. She began to diet without her parents' knowledge, and when she didn't get the desired results as quickly as she wanted, she began to starve herself for long periods of time or would indulge in large quantities of food, then make herself throw up. Unfortunately, this pattern of behavior is all too common for teenagers in today's society. The pressure from media, magazines, boys, television, and society can overcome the tender and maturing esteem of a young girl. In Charlene's case, the Lord revealed to me what she was doing, and together we were able to overcome this setback through prayer and the guidance of the Holy Spirit.

There is a place in society where the size 3 girl is Queen. She is powerful, successful, and in much demand—especially in beauty magazines and high schools across America. Unfortunately, research tells us that eight million people in the United States suffer from eating disorders.[26]

In an interview for the movie *Catwoman,* Halle Berry was asked about her beauty. Her response was both profound and wise:

> Beauty? Let me tell you something. Being thought of as a beautiful woman has spared me nothing in life. Not heartache, not trouble, and love has been difficult. Beauty is essentially meaningless and is always transitory, and I can't believe what people do to themselves, to make themselves look beautiful. . . . Then they end up distorted, where they still have that hole in their soul that led them to change themselves to begin with.

God's Word offers a similar proclamation: "Charm is deceptive, and beauty is fleeting; but a woman who fears the LORD is to be praised" (Proverbs 31:30, NIV). I have always been a fan of Katharine Hepburn. She was one of the most physically beautiful women God ever created. I have kept two pictures of her on my refrigerator for years—one of her in her prime, and the other of her late in life. Those pictures remind me that beauty fades and that we must develop an internal beauty that will radiate Christ to the world even after our physical beauty declines.

Another tactic Satan uses against our children involves abuse and pain. The lasting effects of his attacks on the tender soul of a young child becomes the basis on which he courts them as teens and adults. Let me explain. If children are abandoned by a parent when they are young, as teens they will likely struggle with rejection and identity issues. As a result, Satan will create situations or thoughts that feed or irritate that wound. As that injury festers, Satan is more than willing to encourage an imitation of real peace or relief to numb that wound. His weapons in this area include but are not limited to pornography, eating disorders, money, sex, drugs, alcohol, and homosexuality. This unrighteous "balm" gives wounded children the illusion that they are in control and have the ability to self-soothe through the world. As adults who follow Christ, we know this is a web of deception.

Even childish behavior such as name calling or rejection from peers, if overlooked as "normal" childhood experiences that happen in playschool and elementary education, can cause lifelong wounds. Who can't remember hurtful names they were called in first and second grade? Most of us can still remember the person's name who did it, where they were, and exactly what was said. We remember those things because they left a mark on our forming, impressionable souls. It's important for us as parents and educators to address these problems when they present themselves because if unresolved, these issues can develop defiance and can breed anger toward God and others. Further, a victim mentality can develop, and this sets up wounded individuals for failed relationships in their adult lives and may breed more estrangement from God. The enemy of our souls—imitating God's goodness—then steps in through various sources and promises to fill the void that others have helped create.

One of Satan's most frequent strategies is to offer us internal peace apart from God. Every human being desires such peace. People often refer to their lack of peace as a void that they feel. As parents, we must minister to that void in our children, explaining to them that only the love of Jesus Christ who sacrificed himself for us can fill that emptiness inside them. Everything else we try will lead to a greater emptiness. We need to teach them this from birth, so that when they spread their wings—which they will do—they will find refuge in the Almighty, even if they try first to find it elsewhere.

A WAR FOR YOUR CHILDREN'S SOULS

A battle for your children's souls is taking place, and Satan will use whatever means he can to deceive them into giving them to him. If your children have not yet made a confession of faith, they are property that the enemy is seeking to purchase. "All this I will give you," he says to them, "if you will bow down and worship me." Satan, however, is not telling them the whole story. A fuller, more truthful offering would be: "I will give all this to you if you will bow down and worship me, but only until Jesus comes back. He will at that point utterly defeat me. Then, together with me, you will spend eternity in hell. You will live in the lake of fire prepared for the Devil and his angels, where there is weeping and gnashing of teeth. Your thirst will be unquenchable. You will remain in constant torment. But look at the bright side—you'll have fun while you're here on earth. So how about it? I'll give you the world if you give me your soul. Deal?"

This is why Scripture refers to Satan, the Adversary, as a deceiver. Jesus said that "he is a liar and the father of lies" (John 8:44). The New Testament also refers to him as destroyer, accuser, and murderer (1 Corinthians 10:9-10; Revelation 12:10; John 8:44).

CHRIST'S COURTSHIP OF OUR CHILDREN

When Adam and Eve sinned in the garden, they brought spiritual death into their perfect relationship with God. It's interesting to note that God took the initiative and went looking for them, even as they hid from him. Although they were the ones who caused the division by their disobedience, God pursued them. He also pursues our children.

God doesn't approach our children empty-handed. Despite their rebellion, he comes bearing gifts. He graciously courts them by his Holy Spirit from their birth, offering to raise them from spiritual death to life and promising freedom from the curse of their sin through the redemption of Jesus Christ. He courts and woos them by his Spirit, drawing them to Jesus. As parents, one of our roles is to continually point this process out to our children when we see it occurring.

The person of the Holy Spirit is a gift who has immeasurable power. Jesus referred to him as "the Helper" (John 15:26), or, in Greek, as a *parakletos*, one who is called alongside another to defend, encourage, and comfort. He is referred to as "the Spirit of truth" (John 14:16-17; 15:26; 16:13). He walks beside believers, exposing their need for something more than the world can offer. God comes to us in the Holy Spirit with promises of eternal treasure. The difference between the courtship of God and the courtship of Satan is eminently clear. Satan is a liar and a deceiver; the truth is not in him. God, on the other hand, cannot lie. He is the personification of truth.

God makes thousands of promises to us, his children, throughout the Bible. And he makes good on every promise he makes to us. He does not lie, and he will fulfill every last promise for the believer who walks according to his will.

Just as Satan's names reveal his character, so do God's many names reveal the aspects of his character. He is our Shield, Protector, Creator, Avenger, Healer, Fortress, Deliverer, Rock, Refuge, Provider, Shepherd, Redeemer, and much more.

Most little girls spend their childhoods dreaming of meeting Prince Charming, someone who will love them unconditionally, care for them, protect them, provide for them, and walk beside them. Jesus is that person. Equally so, boys desire to attain these same characteristics and can only do so by retaining a relationship with the ultimate Mentor, God himself.

ALLEGIANCE, RELATIONSHIP, AND OBEDIENCE

The fundamental battle is between the father of lies and the Spirit of truth.

NEIL ANDERSON,
CHRIST-CENTERED THERAPY

From the day our children are born until the moment they die, they are in a spiritual battle, romanced by good and seduced by evil. To teach them anything different is to throw them into a proverbial den of hungry lions without a way to defend themselves. Furthermore, the courtship of Satan does not end with their conversion; we cannot assume that our children are safe from assault merely because they've given their hearts to Christ as their Savior. The Evil One cannot steal their salvation, but he continues to try to turn their hearts toward him and to lure them away from their First Love. He tries to convince them that the one who paid the ransom for them has lied to them and has forsaken them. This is one reason it's important for parents to be honest with their children regarding Santa and the Easter Bunny. They must teach their children the difference between imaginary characters and the true Savior. Our children must know without a doubt that Christ exists and is on their side and is interceding for them every minute of every day.

Satan's goal for us and for our children is spiritual adultery. Consider all the times the Israelites were drawn off task spiritually and served false gods. The Devil knows that if he can get our children to take their eyes away from their First Love, they will become useless to God. Are children really that big of a threat to the enemy of their souls? Absolutely. Some of the most powerful individuals in Christ, who have moved mountains in the spirit realm, are under the age of eighteen! I've seen it myself—adults being prayed for and healed by a child's believing request to God or demons fleeing at the command of an eight-year-old. It happens every day all over the world. It has everything to do with children's faith and knowledge. If they are educated and encouraged to walk in Christ, they will.

There are only two camps in this spiritual war: God's and Satan's. *There is no middle ground.* In order for us to evaluate clearly where our children stand in the spirit realm, we need to understand the truth ourselves and to educate them about the purpose of the war.

HOW THE WAR BEGAN

Isaiah 14 speaks of a spiritual war that raged in the heavenly realm between Christ and Satan, whose name was formerly Lucifer, "angel of light." Lucifer desired to climb up to heaven and place his throne above the highest stars, where he would sit like a king—he would be like God (vv. 13-14). Many theologians have suggested that Lucifer's rebellion was born out of God's decision to create humans above the angels. But Lucifer would not have been satisfied simply to be above humans; he wanted to be above the highest stars, where he would be like God. In fact, Lucifer aspired to rule over God!

Lucifer failed in his rebellion, and God evicted him from the heavenly realm. Since God placed human beings above the angels, including Lucifer, it is plausible to conclude that Satan's goal is still to destroy mankind. Furthermore, in his ongoing rebellion against God he attempts to wound God by destroying his most treasured creation—you and me.

Satan, after his expulsion from heaven, enlisted a hierarchy of angels (his followers) to carry out his evil plan to destroy God's children and the earth that they inhabit. Lucifer's hatred for God's creation has grown ever more destructive as, like a child who is out of control, jealous of a new sibling, and angry with his parents, he continues to press the attack against God and his children. It began with Adam and Eve and continues today. God said in Genesis 3:15 (NIV), "I will put enmity between you and the woman, and between your offspring and hers; he will crush your head, and you will strike his heel."

THE WAR BETWEEN THE SEEDS

The focus of the previous verse is the conflict between the seed of the woman and the seed of the serpent. That battle will continue until the seed of the woman finally crushes the head of the serpent. The serpent could only painfully bruise the heel of the woman's seed. When God speaks of the seed of Satan, his meaning is twofold: one seed of Satan is demons and evil spirits, who are fallen angels and are like Satan in nature. The other seed is unredeemed men and women who bear Satan's nature (see 1 John 3:8, 10, 12). The twofold seed of the woman is the Lord Jesus Christ (see Galatians 3:16; Revelation 12:1-5, 13) as well as redeemed men and women who have accepted Jesus Christ as their Savior.

In Genesis 4 we see the first instance of the age-old opposition between those two seeds. It comes in the form of a satanic attack against the human family. Cain, a son of disobedience, violently murders Abel, the seed of a woman. Satan has been unrelenting in his attacks against the human family ever since. He rallies his seed to attack, destroy, and kill the woman's seed.

THE POWERS THEY ARE UP AGAINST

By God's design, on the other side of the battlefield there is a hierarchy among God's angels, the spirit beings whom we know as archangels, messengers, warriors, and heralds. Scripture refers to fallen angels as rulers, authorities, powers, principalities, and spiritual forces. All angels, whether God's or Satan's, are active in the human arena, but neither side can act on its own authority. There must be permission from a spiritual commander—God or Satan (and Satan can only give such permission as God allows it). And demons cannot invade without a point of entry into the life of the human being who is under attack. This may take the form of a direct invitation or of an opening that is the result of the permission of the person who is in spiritual authority over the victim. Demonic harassment can even take place through a generational entry point—that is, because of past demonic involvement in the family.

It is important to clarify here what we mean by demonic involvement as opposed to demonic possession. Satan cannot "possess" a Christian. Possession implies ownership. When individuals make a commitment to receive Christ as their Savior, they become slaves of Christ, purchased by his blood. Satan has no power to snatch away someone who belongs to God himself. Believers can nevertheless harbor demonic strongholds in various areas of their lives. Such strongholds are the result of granting permission to Satan, through willful submission to sin, to assert his influence in their lives.

As powerful as Satan may be, even to the point of establishing strongholds in the lives of believers, he is virtually impotent. He is not God, who alone is the Creator of all spiritual laws, principles, and structures that exist within the spiritual as well as the natural realm. In order to accomplish his purposes, therefore, the enemy takes what God has already created for good and twists it to his evil intent. Satan counterfeits and perverts the truth at every opportunity. He is a deceiver. Furthermore, since his forgeries have no value, his imitation of God's truth is short-lived. Lies are empty and unfulfilling. Still, Satan counterfeits God's work in order to enslave individuals. He is the original Jekyll and Hyde, masquerading as an angel of light to hide his true identity (2 Corinthians 11:14). But his blessings soon turn to curses, with darkness replacing the light and death consuming the life he has promised.

Fortunately, God's power and Satan's are unequal. God's power is superior; Satan's is subordinate. God limits Satan's power. Still, the Evil One is immensely powerful. The genocide that took place during the Holocaust provides ample evidence of the demonic influence and power one person can wield when he is sold out to Satan. Over six million of God's chosen people died because one man, Adolf Hitler, willingly became a pawn of the Evil One. He led millions of human beings to cooperate with the satanic kingdom. The spirit world and the natural world are connected. What we do on earth yields spiritual consequences.

We can trace this all the way back to the beginning. Eve misled her husband, Adam, who relinquished to Satan his position as lord of the earth. Adam and Eve thus lost their intimate relationship with God and were thrown out of the garden, the only place where the spiritual and earthly realms were in complete harmony. The choices we make affect our spiritual relationship with God and Satan, as well as our physical lives.

THIS PRESENT DARKNESS

When we drive into certain cities, we sense a spirit of darkness. While witchcraft, prostitution, suicide, satanic worship, murder, and other hideous crimes occur in every town, some cities emanate a blatant demonic presence. Even a hotel room in which ungodly activities have occurred can become a dwelling place for evil spirits. In some cities, towns, counties, states, and even entire nations, many people have given themselves over to Satan. Satanic strongholds begin with one individual who is willing to set aside God's will in order to fulfill his lusts. Like an infectious disease, this person travels to other receptive people until entire families and geographic regions become entrapped.

This was especially apparent to me during a trip to eastern Europe in 2004. I taught spiritual warfare principles to missionary parents and their children in Budapest, Hungary. The Iron Curtain had fallen years earlier, but the spirit of Communism was still alive and well in that city. The moment I arrived, I sensed a spirit of oppression. It was evident in the way the city's inhabitants responded to one another and to the missionaries ministering there. Their attitude of hopelessness was manifested in everything, including their homes, attire, and faces. There were no children playing in open areas, and when you saw a child, he or she sat quietly looking at the ground in sadness. It obviously would take more than the falling of the Iron Curtain to set these people free.

KNOWING WHERE OUR CHILDREN STAND

Before we can ever hope to teach our children about spiritual warfare, we must explore and find out which Captain they are currently serving—God or Satan. Three indicators reveal the spiritual camp in which they are living:

1. *Allegiance.* To whom do they give their allegiance? Matthew 7:16 tells us that the "fruit" of individuals' behavior indicates whom they serve. Children who listen to ungodly music, dress inappropriately, curse, and live a worldly life have pledged their allegiance to the Devil. I'm not saying this is a conscious effort on their part—they are deceived. But by allowing our children to partake of such filth, we become spiritually responsible.

2. *Relationship.* Have our children made a confession of faith? Do they belong to the family of God? If not, our primary goal as parents should be to pray and do warfare so our children will come to know Christ as their Savior.

3. *Obedience.* Whom are our children obeying? Most parents are pretty good at teaching their children morals. The problem with morals is, they are predominantly designed around consensus. If the majority of people agree that it's wrong to murder another person, then murder is wrong. However, if the majority rule that premarital sex is okay, then it's not morally wrong to engage in it before marriage, we are told. Just look at how society has changed in the last fifty years. What was morally unacceptable in our parents' day has become permissible today. Our children must learn to be obedient to God's ways.

When allegiance to Christ's kingdom, a personal relationship with Christ, and obedience to Christ are absent, the only alternative is to live in allegiance, relationship, and obedience to Satan. There is no middle ground. It must be one or the other. Our children cannot serve themselves without turning their backs on God and facing the gates of hell. They must choose between two commanders, and they must decide whom they will serve. Luke 16:13 (NIV) says, "No servant can serve two masters. Either he will hate the one and love the other, or he will be devoted to the one and despise the other." Matthew 12:25

(NIV) tells us, "Every kingdom divided against itself will be ruined . . . [it] will not stand." You can't get any clearer than that!

Children who straddle the fence that separates God's kingdom and Satan's are in big trouble. They are married to Christ but flirt adulterously with Satan. Revelation 3:15-16 warns us, "you are neither cold nor hot. Would that you were either cold or hot! So, because you are lukewarm, and neither hot nor cold, I will spit you out of my mouth." We must teach our children allegiance to Christ and encourage them never to look back or consider the other side.

Joshua called the Israelites to make a decision about their allegiances. He told them they must choose today whom they would serve (Joshua 24:15). Our kids have to make choices similar to theirs. Have your children chosen whom they will serve? Where does their allegiance lie? To whom are they related? Are they obeying God's Word? Examining the answers to these questions will give you a good foundation of where to start ministering to your child. Once you know, you will be ready to enter basic training with your child, where together you will learn the dynamics of spiritual battle.

7

THE HOLY SPIRIT: OUR CHILDREN'S EVER-PRESENT COMPANION

Live by the Spirit, and you will not gratify the desires of the sinful nature.

GALATIANS 5:16, NIV

The Holy Spirit is the most instrumental partner a parent can have when doing spiritual warfare, and the greatest gift we can help our children unwrap in their own lives. If you comprehend the power of the Holy Spirit, you will learn everything that you need to know as he leads and guides you in your role as a parent. Without the Holy Spirit there can be no victory. The Holy Spirit goes before us and enables us to do all things through Christ who strengthens us.

The Holy Spirit is a parent's most reliable source of help in teaching his or her children defensive and offensive strategies. Apart from him, neither you nor your children have hope for success on the battlefield. He provides direction, wisdom, truth, clarity, strength, and knowledge even of the underlying motives of the enemy.

OUR HELPER AND OUR BREATH

Jesus referred to the Holy Spirit as "the Helper" (John 14:26; 15:26; 16:7), which refers to one who is called alongside another. Like God the Father and God the Son, the Holy Spirit is omniscient (all-knowing), omnipresent (present everywhere), and omnipotent (all-powerful). His role is to create, convict, regenerate, baptize, fill, and empower believers. He indwells, teaches, guides, and intercedes for us. These are the attributes of the One who comes alongside us.

When we rely on him to guide us, we are accessing the power of God! As powerful as he is, however, we must resist the temptation to picture him as a kind of Terminator spirit. He is also gentle, patient, joyful, kind, faithful, and self-controlled. What a beautiful contrast! The Spirit of God is the everlasting breath of God. In fact, the word translated "Spirit" in the New Testament comes from the Greek word *pneuma*, which also means "breath."

Genesis 2:7 tells us that when the Lord formed man from the dust of the ground, he "breathed into his nostrils the breath of life." Likewise, at your child's birth, he (or she) broke the silence with a strident cry as he took his first breath—the gift of a breath that he received from God himself.

We could do without many things in this world, but we cannot live without the breath of God. We can fast, abstaining from food and drink for days, or deprive ourselves of earthly pleasures, denying our passions, and still live. We cannot, however, live without breath. A person may hold his breath for a while, even to the point of losing consciousness. At that point, however, he will begin to breathe spontaneously.

It is the breath of our Almighty Creator that gives us life and enables the rest of our anatomy to function. We cannot live without it. God is life, and life is in his breath. Therefore, we cannot live without him. Do you see the necessity of having him in our lives?

The Holy Spirit has been active in our children's lives ever since the day they were born. When they were unbelievers, the Holy Spirit courted their souls, revealing their need for something more than their earthly existence, which they found to be so unsatisfying. In response to his wooing, they accepted the gift of salvation and received the gift of the Holy Spirit, or "Helper," to assist them on their journey toward intimacy with Christ. It is our responsibility as parents to point this out to our children and to help them understand what a divine gift the Holy Spirit is to those who trust in him.

Many children are unwittingly taught to place the Holy Spirit in a box and open it only on Sunday mornings. By their parents' example, the Holy Spirit is downgraded from a member of the Trinity to someone who simply gives believers "warm fuzzies." As a result, many children become dissatisfied and begin to see their faith in God as merely an emotional experience and not the supernatural transformation that God promised. God never intended us to place his Holy Spirit—God's very breath—in a spiritual box, used only occasionally. His role is to be a Helper, walking beside our children as their ever-present companion and aiding them in battle.

CONVERSATION WITH THE HOLY SPIRIT

When the Bible tells us to pray without ceasing (1 Thessalonians 5:17), that is not an unattainable challenge meant to discourage us. Rather, it is an encouragement for us to continue walking in the Spirit and to engage in ongoing conversation with him. It is not difficult to pray without ceasing. We naturally engage in conversation with a person who walks with us, don't we? There are times of silence, but only because we are listening. We are continually to bring our conversation under the submission of the Holy Spirit for a check of what claims to be truth.

When we converse with the Holy Spirit in regard to our children, he uncovers their motives, revealing their options for Christlike living. Further, he shows us where and how to apply the balm of Gilead in their lives. As you begin to function within this relationship as a spiritual guardian to your children, you will see a relationship of sheer beauty evolve between you and the Spirit. When we are able to assist our children to see the Holy Spirit in this way, we are empowering them to call on the powerful name of God in all circumstances. Because he is faithful, our children will learn to hear his voice and to distinguish it from their own, and from the misleading words of the enemy. This will develop the discernment that they have had at least in embryo, so to speak, from physical birth.

When believers talk about discernment, they are talking about special understanding from the Holy Spirit, that is, seeing others and situations with spiritual eyes. This can come in the form of a picture, a word, or simply a feeling. Few people have actually heard God speak to them in an audible voice. It is more frequently a prompting, a silent whisper in the mind, or a strong sensation in the soul. Discernment is an ability that we develop through an ever-deepening intimacy with God. We all have discernment at birth, but the world and our environment hold back our ability to hear his promptings. Our sin also interferes.

When we engage in a relationship with the Holy Spirit, he offers to us the gift of intimacy, which further results in the ability to discern. In this intimate relationship, our children build trust, becoming sure of God's promises, and begin to live out this relationship through faith. Naturally we want our children to experience intimacy of this kind. We want them to truly grasp the power available through the Holy Spirit and allow them to see him working in their lives.

When Jesus was leaving his earthly life, he gave the Holy Spirit to us as believers as a gift throughout our lives. He said:

> *It is to your advantage that I go away; for if I do not go away, the Helper will not come to you; but if I depart, I will send Him to you . . . when He, the Spirit of truth, has come, He will guide you into all truth; for He will not speak on His own authority, but whatever He hears He will speak; and He will tell you things to come. He will glorify Me, for He will take of what is Mine and declare it to you. All things that the Father has are Mine. Therefore I said that He will take of Mine and declare it to you.*
>
> JOHN 16:7, 13-15, NKJV

Jesus promised his disciples that although he was leaving this world, he would never abandon them. He would always be with them in the person of the Holy Spirit, who is equal to both God the Father and God the Son. The Holy Spirit will infuse our children with the strength they need to live for Christ in the midst of daily battles and with the ability to bear the fruit of Christlike virtues. When they receive the gift of the Holy Spirit, they are in a real sense also receiving God the Father and God the Son. In doing so, they have at their disposal a major arsenal of power.

TO GRIEVE OR NOT TO GRIEVE

The Holy Spirit dwells in our believing children's hearts and empowers them to serve the Lord. Although the Holy Spirit enters their lives to help them live for God, he does not turn them into robots. They will constantly battle the sin nature and will at times fail miserably. When our children willfully continue to sin, however, they "grieve" the Holy Spirit (Ephesians 4:30). The believer who walks with the Holy Spirit will immediately recognize this grieving of the Holy Spirit. We need to talk to our children about what that feels like within us, so they can identify with it within their own hearts. We then need to help them recognize when they have sinned, repent of it, accept God's truth, and turn away from that behavior in the future. But that is not the end of this teaching opportunity. We need to further explore with them what happens if they run from that grieving.

When we grieve the Holy Spirit, we often ignore his grieving in our souls. Like a five-year-old child who doesn't want to hear what someone else is saying, we plug our spiritual ears and scream, "I can't hear you!" The danger is that in extreme circumstances many people mask this grieving with alcohol, drugs, spending, sex, or food, to mention just a few. The sin in which we have participated seems at the time more rewarding than the freedom that accompanies walking in Christ. Sin *is* pleasurable for a season. But then like sour milk it curdles in our spirits, and we long to rid our spirits of it. This can be a never-ending cycle of events in our children's lives if we don't teach them how to stop the cycle with repentance and righteousness.

When our children come face-to-face with sin, they have a choice: they can nurture it in order to fill a felt need, thereby eventually creating a stronghold for the enemy, or they can submit their felt needs to the Holy Spirit, who will fill that need with truth.

I want to encourage you to allow your children to make the wrong decisions at times. In doing so they will experience natural consequences and will learn for themselves to identify what has happened in their souls. I'm not saying you should advise them to do something wrong. What I am saying is that always intervening for them and telling them to do something "just because you said so" carries little understanding of the process of sin and restoration. When sin occurs—and it will—talk openly about what they are experiencing internally and how to correct the error.

Our children must come to understand that to have the Holy Spirit with us and in us is a great privilege. It is also a great responsibility to listen to him and then respond in a godly way. When we ignore the Holy Spirit, we are ignoring God, and we are no longer receptive to any change. On the other hand, when we gladly permit the Holy Spirit to lead and guide us, we flourish!

The Holy Spirit is like a compass that guides our children. In fact, I often give compasses to children when I teach them this lesson. We explore together how a compass works and how the Holy Spirit leads us in the correct direction. I further explain the benefits that relying on the Holy Spirit will bring to them. I tell them:

- He will be your teacher (John 16:13).
- He will intercede on your behalf (Romans 8:26).
- He will comfort you (John 14:16).
- He will sanctify you—that is, he will set you apart for a special purpose (2 Thessalonians 2:13).
- He will convict you—he will make you aware of sin (John 16:8-11).
- He will accomplish regeneration (or new life) in you (John 3:6).
- He will guide you into all truth (John 16:13).
- He will convince you of the truth of the gospel (John 16:8, 13-14).
- He will empower you to witness (Acts 1:8; 4:31; 1 Peter 1:12).
- He will destroy the power of sin in your life (Romans 8:2-6).
- He will lead and even control your life (Romans 8:14; Galatians 5:16, 25).
- He will dwell in you (John 14:17).
- He will remind you of what Jesus said (John 14:26).
- He confirms your salvation (Romans 8:16; 1 John 3:24; 4:13).

• He gives you life (Romans 8:5-11).

• He gives you joy (Acts 13:52; Romans 14:17).

• He gives you hope (Romans 15:13; 1 Thessalonians 1:3).

• He liberates you (Romans 8:1-2).

• He gives you strength to overcome sin (Romans 8:9-11; Galatians 5:16).

• He seals your inheritance in Christ (2 Corinthians 1:22; Ephesians 1:13-14).

• He speaks through you (Matthew 10:19-20).

• He teaches you (Luke 12:11-12; John 14:26; 1 Corinthians 2:13).

• He testifies to you about Jesus (John 15:26; 1 John 5:6).

• He guides you (John 16:13; Acts 8:29; 10:19; 16:6; Romans 8:14).

• He strengthens and encourages you (Acts 9:31).

• He loves others through you (Romans 5:5).

• He produces righteous fruit in you (Galatians 5:22-23).

• He helps you pray (Romans 8:26-27).

• He helps you worship (Ephesians 5:18-19; Philippians 3:3).

• He gives you spiritual gifts (1 Corinthians 12:7-11).

• He edifies your spirit (Ephesians 3:16; Jude 20).

• He unites believers (Ephesians 4:3-4; Philippians 2:1-2).

• He strengthens you with power so Christ will dwell in your heart (Ephesians 3:16-17).

• He gave you the spirit of sonship (Romans 8:15-16).

When both parents and children live in dependence on God's Spirit, they will discover that God will provide every tool that they need in order to accomplish his will. Do you see the power that accompanies this precious gift to your children? Through the Spirit, they can do all things. Apart from him, they can do nothing.

The apostle Paul prayed in the first chapter of his letter to the Colossian church a petition that I wish we as parents would pray over our children daily. He prayed that believers would have "spiritual wisdom and understanding" (v. 9). The word translated "spiritual" means "by the assistance of the Holy Spirit." "Wisdom" refers to "skill, tact, aptitude, and expertise in trade," but in this verse it is "spiritual" wisdom—moral discernment, the fear of the Lord, and so on. This petition is needed in spiritual warfare as you and your child access the power of heaven that resides within you both through the Holy Spirit. My prayer for you is that you will rely on the Holy Spirit, who is eager to assist you in your teaching role. May you walk in step with the Spirit so that you can engage in spiritual battle with great skill and train your children to do the same.

THE DYNAMICS OF
BATTLE

All those gathered here will know that it is not by sword or spear that the LORD saves; for the battle is the LORD's, and he will give all of you into our hands.

1 SAMUEL 17:47, NIV

I took a couple of chapters to talk about the glaring issues within the lives of today's children and their parents and the different tactics Satan uses to ensnare both. Now I feel it's time to clarify that I do not believe there is a demon behind every bush waiting to attack our children when we or they least expect it. Equally so, I want to emphasize that our children are not without assault twenty-four hours a day. Let me explain these seemingly contradictory statements.

The Bible talks about two other enemies besides Satan and his cohorts that seek to destroy our children—the world and their own sin nature. Both are selfish and potentially spiritually destructive. Our flesh or sin nature consists of the totality of our core beliefs, desires, and needs apart from Jesus that are relentlessly self-centered and deceptive above all things. The world is comprised of millions of people who operate according to this fleshly standpoint. When you look beyond the research and statistics I revealed in the previous chapters, you will find both components—the flesh and the world. Since the fall in the Garden of Eden, in conjunction with satanic influence, these works have led to moral deterioration in the lives of today's youths. Therefore, spiritual warfare must be multidimensional.

In addition to attacks from the world, Satan, and our flesh, we must also consider that there are times in life when the Lord allows his children to be tested. Sometimes this testing can look and feel like an assault from the enemy of our souls. So how can we tell the difference?

When Satan attacks believers, it most commonly includes confusion, accusations, feelings of rejection, condemnation, discouragement, and hopelessness. Additionally, when relentless and not addressed in the spirit realm, his attacks can lead to depression. Generally the Devil's assault is aimed at deteriorating your child's integrity, character, or esteem in Christ. His attacks are also often persistent, giving the assaulted believer no choice but to accept the attack or stand against it in the name of Jesus. Rarely can one run from a satanic assault.

God's testing is different from Satan's attacks in several ways. First, when being tested by the Lord, there is no confusion associated with it, but rather clarity about the situation. We are able to see clearly that we have a choice to make. We must decide to walk in faith and believe God's Word and promises or to walk away from the truth. God's testing does not tear down our identity but affirms it. So we do not run from it but can stand firm while we're being tested as we walk according to his will. Whenever we are tested by the Lord, there is a promise of spiritual growth. When God tests us, he does so only after he is confident that we know the right choice already. It's like a test in school—we learn about a specific topic all week, then have a pop quiz. We know the answer; the question is, are we going to do the right thing on the test?

When our flesh is battling us, the only choice we have is either to cave into its desires or stand firm! Fleshly temptations are usually obsessive and stem from a desire, craving, or yearning. Our flesh craves sin to which we have opened doors in the past. For example, once our body has experienced the pleasure of sex, it desires more. In the context of a godly relationship under the marriage covenant, that's not a bad thing. However, outside God's will it will lead to spiritual ruin. To desire sex is a godly passion, and we must not condemn it but instead not dwell on it until the appropriate time.

An attack from the world is external. We can always run away from a worldly assault. As a matter of fact, Scripture admonishes us to flee from such attacks (1 Corinthians 6:18; 10:14; 1 Timothy 6:9-11; 2 Timothy 2:22). Assaults from the world include pressure to conform to its likeness and often feed on one of our five senses—sight, hearing, touch, smell, taste.

When assaulted, it's important that we first look at who the perpetrator is and consider whether it's a test from the Lord. This will determine how we ought to respond. Let's consider how we should respond to a fleshly attack and how to teach our children to do the same.

Our flesh is the only aspect of war that we battle over which we have any direct control. Our flesh is hard enough to battle within our own bodies; so to spiritually intervene for our children is an even tougher crusade. This is because their flesh is made up of several components—their core beliefs about how they see themselves, how they see others, how they think others see them, how they see God, and how they think God sees them.[27] Children's core beliefs highly affect their will and desires.

These core beliefs are generally the result of events—real or perceived—that our children experience during their early years. One of the developmental stages that children go through involves the belief that the world revolves around them. When my infant grandson Dallin has a need, he cries. My daughter then meets his need, whether by feeding him, changing him, or simply holding him. As far as Dallin is concerned, the sun rises and sets because of him. This is a normal part of his development, and it will take a couple of years for him to realize that he is not the center of the universe.

Children's core beliefs can be twisted when they experience trauma or negative family events. The result can be guilt, shame, or a false sense of responsibility. Without spiritual intervention, it is likely they will carry these feelings into adulthood.

Our minds are like computer hard drives loaded with memories. If you were abused as a child, it is not the abuse itself that keeps you in bondage. Rather, what keeps you imprisoned are the lies or core beliefs about yourself and others that are a result of the abuse. Our core beliefs are built on our childhood perspectives of various events. Those beliefs change only when we confront them with the truth and when, in faith, we choose to walk according to the truth.

Children lack the reasoning skills needed to defeat unhealthy circumstances, words, and actions that damage them until they are somewhere between twelve and eighteen years of age.[28] Consequently, they unconsciously form negative core beliefs. Dr. Ed Murphy, author of the book *The Handbook on Spiritual Warfare* and Professor of Divinity at Biola University, states:

> If we have lies stored in our experiential knowledge we will have little choice but to act out accordingly or else live in a life of constant struggle and self-effort. Mental darkness cripples the spirit; since we can only act as far as we can think, our spirit person (our real self) cannot live out its righteousness until the mind is free from unrighteous lies. Therefore, only when we purge our minds from lies can we live and act in the freedom of Christ.[29]

When we have a child who is consistently responding negatively to the same situation, we must explore, through conversation with him or her, his or her core belief regarding that problem. I grew up in a home with an abusive father and with a mother who was unable to stand up to him without physical, mental, and emotional repercussions. As a result I developed distorted core beliefs about men and women. I believed that all men are abusive and that all women are weak and helpless. Although core beliefs may be true, they often are not. These core beliefs were formed in an abusive environment, and I held them for many years. Without God's intervention, our negative core beliefs control us, sending us into a downward and destructive spiritual spiral.

Our Creator made each of us different, unique, special, irreplaceable. And yet we are also similar. One way we are like others is that all humanity follows the same basic cognitive mental process in decision-making.

1. We perceive an event with one of our five senses—smell, taste, hearing, sight, or touch.

2. We have specific thoughts about the event: we reject it or justify it.

3. We experience any of a number of emotions.

4. We respond by choosing a course of action.

Every human being goes through this process, whether consciously or unconsciously, multiple times each day. It's in our genetic blueprint. Our understanding of this process and teaching it to our children is vital to spiritual warfare because it will help us sort out our child's motives and beliefs and will help us understand how to advocate on their behalf and how to help them overcome difficulties. Let's examine in greater detail each step of the decision-making process. We begin with the events of life that we perceive with our five senses.

OUR PERCEPTIONS

The cognitive or mental process that occurs in all of us is the first step that occurs in facing any situation in life and is based solely on our perception or core beliefs about specific events. Our minds kick off this process automatically by receiving a thought about what is going on around us. For example, let's say an eight-year-old girl is standing with her family in the living room when her father slaps her on the bottom and jokingly says she's getting fat. This event automatically causes the child to think a thought such as *I'm fat* or *Daddy thinks I'm fat*. This thought may or may not be true. Regardless of its truth, her perception is that he thinks she's fat, which leads her to think she's overweight. These thoughts stimulate the child's emotions, then their response. If not corrected in this child's mind, it can become a core belief.

From a spiritual standpoint, a core belief is a thought that the individual has received into his or her being and over which he or she has taken personal ownership. It has become a part of that person and is one part in his or her individuality. Core beliefs are generally rooted in childhood experiences and remain until they are uprooted and replaced with truth. Spiritually healthy core beliefs need not be uprooted, of course, but instead watered frequently.

The cognitive process occurs hundreds of times a day regardless of the occurring situations or events. There need not be a crisis for this process to be kicked into action. I wish we as parents could control the events that happen in our children's lives, but we can't, nor can we teach them to do so. But we can teach them to look at those events differently—from a biblical perspective. We must learn to analyze the events objectively and teach our children to do the same, so we can engage in battle individually and as a family with the appropriate weapons found in God's Word.

Each person perceives events differently. Six different people can watch the same accident occur and recall it in six different ways. The same six people will have a different perception of the event because of their core beliefs. The way we perceive an event determines our emotional, mental, physical, and spiritual responses.

One question that is important to consider when looking at a specific event is whether or not it may be a temptation from the flesh, a trial from God, or a spiritual attack from the enemy. It's important to understand that we are not primarily human beings in a spirit world but spirit beings in a human world, and we must maintain that perspective when examining life and defending ourselves.

It is not always easy to recognize negative core beliefs in our own lives because the primary strategy of the Devil is deceit. Unlike temptation and accusation from the enemy, his deception is subtle. Satan misleads and misdirects us so that we believe a lie to be the truth. Satan deceived Eve. She believed what he was telling her, and the deception yielded disastrous consequences for her and all her descendants. If you are having difficulty identifying specific negative core beliefs in your children's lives, consider for a moment ongoing behaviors they have that are not healthy. Do they lie? Overexaggerate? Not do their homework? Cheat? Gossip? Whatever the negative or ungodly behavior is, if it is done persistently, there is a negative core belief behind it.

It is important to recognize negative core beliefs because they affect our thoughts. By recognizing them we take the first step in establishing the foundation of repentance and reshaping our core beliefs or perceptions. Once we identify these in our children's lives, we need to talk with them about their validity and importance. In doing so, the first step to change is getting them to admit that they have been deceived with some of these beliefs. They must take whatever they have placed above God, put it beneath his control, and place him back on the throne where he belongs. In order to live and walk in core beliefs based on truth, they must recognize that Jesus is truth (see John 14:6), his Word is truth (see John 17:17), the Holy Spirit will guide us into all truth (see John 16:13), and the truth will set us free (see John 8:32).

OUR THOUGHTS

Crises, conflicts, and difficult circumstances are inevitable. People in crisis tend to show poor judgment, act recklessly, get angry, and become argumentative. The way we respond to any given event will direct our lives for better or worse. One type of event to which we must learn to respond properly is temptation.

Each of us experiences temptation, an enticement to sin that arises from human desires and passions (see James 1:14; 1 John 2:16). Enticement may also be from the Devil, who is called "the tempter" (see Matthew 4:3).

The Bible teaches that God does not tempt us (see James 1:13). He does, however, allow us to be tested by circumstances and by the enemy of our souls. Such testing helps us grow in our obedience, in our reliance on him, and in our commitment to his cause. The Lord also promises to provide a way of escape and will not allow us to be tempted beyond what we are able to bear (see 1 Corinthians 10:13). When we submit to God and resist the tempter, the enemy flees from us (see James 4:7).

The key to avoiding defeat is to take every thought captive and make it obedient to Christ (see 2 Corinthians 10:5) before we respond to any given event. That requires us to reframe our core beliefs. Ungodly thoughts are the results of negative core beliefs we have retained from previous experiences, or they might be a result of words or pictures that Satan places in our minds.

A battle is raging in our children's minds between God's truth and their distorted core beliefs. We can teach them to find victory by taking every thought captive to Christ, which means to submit their actions and thoughts to his truth. To submit ourselves is to place ourselves under the authority of another. In order to do that, our children must first acknowledge the lie or idol that has captivated their minds. They can then confess and renounce the lie, accepting the truth of what God has said. How does this work in real life?

Consider my previous example about the young girl who was slapped on her bottom by her dad and told jokingly that she was getting fat. Let's say he did that often and that there were also other times when people were careless in their words toward her natural development into womanhood, and as a result the girl began to see herself as fat, a harmful core belief about herself. As a result, she spent her adolescent and teen years struggling with her identity and weight.

In order for this young adult to heal from this negative core belief, she has to first understand and embrace what God says in his Word about her identity. Then she has to renounce the lie, the negative core belief, and continually repeat the truths found in God's Word until they replace the lie she's been told. In doing so, she will more than likely be bombarded by thoughts from hell, the media, and her own flesh that will feed the pain of her father's words, but with consistency and faith in God's Word her thoughts about herself will change.

The apostle Paul counsels in Philippians 4:8, "whatever is true, whatever is honorable, whatever is just, whatever is pure, whatever is lovely, whatever is commendable, if there is any excellence, if there is anything worthy of praise, think about these things." That is not to say that we can rid ourselves of negative thoughts by simply ignoring them. Rather, we must let Christ's peace rule in our hearts by letting his words dwell richly within us (see Colossians 3:15-16). Our children can overcome lies by choosing to focus on the truth so that it replaces the negative thoughts or core beliefs.

Throughout this process we must remain alert to a serious roadblock—our children's own desires. Sinful desire feeds on pain and selfishness. James 1:14-15 tells us, "But each person is tempted when he is lured and enticed by his own desire. Then desire when it has conceived gives birth to sin, and sin when it is fully grown brings forth death."

The Greek word translated "desire" means "deep longing." It is often an impulsive craving and an ardent pursuit of what is forbidden.

Another term for it is *lust*. Our desires have the power to lead us down a pathway of trouble and death. We can recognize desire in our children when we notice them trying to justify thoughts that are contrary to God's Word. Desire can even motivate them to rip God's Word out of context, misinterpret it, and justify some sin. I recently heard a homosexual priest who was advocating same-sex marriage say, "The Bible talks about an intimate relationship between David and Jonathan. David said he loved him closer than a brother. They were sexually involved." That priest correctly noted that David loved Jonathan but incorrectly interpreted their love as a homosexual relationship, which the Bible expressly forbids. The priest was reading his own meaning into God's Word in an attempt to justify his own sinful desire.

One can only imagine the battle between truth and lies that was taking place in the soul of that priest. We may attempt to justify our sin, but the Holy Spirit will not let us so easily get away with that self-deception. He will make the believer wrestle in his spirit until he is willing to call sin what it is—sin. This internal turmoil will ultimately lead our children either into the counseling office for help or into the hospital for treatment of the resulting illnesses. Many sick individuals (whether mentally, emotionally, spiritually, or physically) are people who are ill because of their own sin!

Another way to justify sin is to minimize it. Who hasn't heard a child say, "Oh, that isn't a lie. It's partly true," or "It's just a little white lie," or "It's no big deal." My son once stole a five-cent token from an arcade. I was appalled as I watched him slowly steal the coin from a distracted adult at the game next to his. After he took it, I pulled him aside. His response was, "It's only worth a nickel!" My response (after a few other words of wisdom) was, "Nickels turn into dollar bills, money turns into CD's, and music turns into cars." It seemed extreme to him to link stealing a nickel to thievery of a vehicle, but I've worked in the prison system for many years with kids. Every one of them began manipulating, stealing, and controlling circumstances and people at a very early age. Sin breeds more sin.

A very good friend of mine was married and flirting with another woman. When I confronted him about it, he said, "I can look at the menu—I just can't order from it." I used his menu analogy to challenge him. "What happens when you're physically hungry and you look at items on a menu that you know you shouldn't eat?" I asked. "Your mouth starts watering, your craving to satisfy your hunger intensifies, and sooner or later you cave in to that desire."

My friend ignored my concern, and within three months he was in an adulterous relationship, separated from his mate, and filing for divorce with the intention of marrying his lover. He moved in with the other woman for six months before discovering that *she* was cheating on *him*. They broke up, and he went back to his spouse, begging for her forgiveness and seeking reconciliation. But the damage was too great. My friend lost his spouse, the custody of his children, and his self-respect and integrity.

A third way you'll find your children justifying their sin is by comparing it to the actions of other kids. They may say, "Well, Johnny does it" or "He hit me first!" or "I only lied about it. Cindy lied and cheated!" We must always regard our children's sin in light of the Bible, God's standard, not in light of worldly or human standards or even our own behavior when we were their age. Just because others cheat on their taxes does not give us the right to do so as adults. Equally so, just because someone else's child gets away with sin doesn't mean ours should or will. Sin is sin and always produces negative consequences, and especially separation from God, our eternal lifeline. We must, therefore, teach our children what the Bible says about different circumstances and help them bring their thoughts into submission to God's truth.

Only then will our children be able to resist the Devil (see James 4:7). If they try to resist the Devil without first submitting to God, the enemy of their souls will chew them up and spit them out. Jesus said, "If you hold to my teaching, you are really my disciples. Then you will know the truth, and the truth will set you free" (John 8:31-32, NIV). Freedom from the attacks of Satan, the world, and our own desires begins with knowing and obeying God's truth.

Once we have taken our thoughts captive, we begin to resist the Devil, and he does not have control over us. Actively choosing to bind our thoughts and hold them accountable to God's Word gives us the upper hand over the lies of the enemy. The battle dynamic of taking our thoughts captive is crucial because our emotions and responses follow our thoughts.

Our child's perceptions and thoughts are only part of the equation. We also must consider their emotions. The way they feel about their experiences deeply influences their cognitive process.

OUR EMOTIONS

The word *emotion* comes from the Latin word *emovere*, meaning literally "to move or displace." Emotions arise from mental stimuli or thoughts that have a symbolic meaning to the person experiencing them. Those symbolic meanings then lead to an action. Researchers generally identify twelve fundamental emotions, nine unpleasant and three pleasant:

UNPLEASANT	PLEASANT
Sorrow	Love
Fear	Joy
Anger	Awe
Jealousy	
Shame	
Disgust	
Pain	
Confusion	
Emptiness	

Emotions are the by-products of what we think, believe, and understand to be true. It has been said that our emotions lie to us; therefore they cannot be trusted. But that is not really the case. What lies to us is our *thoughts*. Emotions flow from the core of our being, and they reflect the wonder of our creation in the image of God. Emotions are not our enemies; rather, they alert us to things that are going on in our minds. God himself expresses a wide range of emotions. He is a passionate God and feels grief when we rebel. He is angry when we make idols of our possessions (Numbers 32:10). But God also delights when we return to him. Because we are made in his image, we also experience those feelings.

Jesus experienced a wide variety of emotions. He felt compassion when he met a leper and when a funeral procession passed by. He felt love when a rich young ruler came to him, anger when the disciples tried to keep little children from him, grief at the time of Lazarus' death, and deep sorrow over the unbelief of his own people, the Jews.

We too experience a wide range of emotions. Unfulfilled dreams and loss inevitably create emotional pain. Consider Hannah, who in 1 Samuel 1 had a loving and devoted husband but experienced pain because of her deep yearning for a child. Scripture tells us that she wept, restricted her appetite, and was depressed (v. 7). She experienced "bitterness of soul" and "grief" (vv. 10, 16, NIV). But Hannah cried out to her God and shared her sorrow with him and with Eli, the priest who stood nearby. Eli then in turn invoked God's blessing on her, a blessing that God fulfilled by granting her a child.

Our emotions are important parts of who we are and of who our children are, but we cannot let them lead our children's behavior. That would be like driving without a map! The directions they must use are in God's Word, and it's our job as parents to teach them how to read the map. Without the intervention of taking their thoughts captive, they will repeatedly replay old tapes from core beliefs, causing their emotions to flare up like an open flame on which life's challenges pour gasoline. If our children do not learn this process now, they will spiral out of control when their hormones start to change at various times in life.

The way we perceive events affects the way we think, which produces any number of a dozen basic emotions. The final component in the cognitive process is our response—the course of action we choose to take.

OUR RESPONSE

Our response to any given situation is in direct correlation to our emotions. *Feelings* are to *response* as *steering wheel* is to *car*. We may not initially recognize the cycle of thought, emotion, and response that leads to our behavior, but it is something we can learn. I grew up in a home in which my father was repeatedly unfaithful to my mother. I was aware of his many infidelities. People gossiped about his behavior. For a time one of his lovers even shared my bedroom with me when I was not more than ten or eleven. In turn, one of the core beliefs that formed in me as an adolescent was that all men are unfaithful and unworthy of trust.

That core belief stayed with me, even later in life after I had married. Whenever my husband arrived home late from work or was absent when I thought he should be home, even when he was simply having lunch with a male friend, I accused him of infidelity. I spent hours crying and dwelling on the belief that he was cheating. After all, every man cheats, right? But he never did. How was I able eventually to move beyond this cycle of defeat and into a cycle of success? It was through the teachings of Scripture.

The Bible's instruction concerning freedom through spiritual warfare is based on the word *stand*. Consider the following verses:

Stand firm and you will see the deliverance the LORD *will bring you today. (Exodus 14:13, NIV)*

You will not need to fight in this battle. Stand firm, hold your position, and see the salvation of the LORD *on your behalf. (2 Chronicles 20:17)*

He lifted me out of the slimy pit, out of the mud and mire; he set my feet on a rock and gave me a firm place to stand. (Psalm 40:2, NIV)

If you do not stand firm in your faith, you will not stand at all. (Isaiah 7:9, NIV)

Therefore, my dear brothers, stand firm. Let nothing move you. (1 Corinthians 15:58, NIV)

Be on your guard; stand firm in the faith; be men [and women] of courage; be strong. (1 Corinthians 16:13, NIV)

For freedom Christ has set us free; stand firm therefore, and do not submit again to a yoke of slavery. (Galatians 5:1)

Therefore take up the whole armor of God, that you may be able to withstand in the evil day, and having done all, to stand firm. Stand therefore. (Ephesians 6:13-14)

So then . . . stand firm and hold to the teachings we passed on to you. (2 Thessalonians 2:15, NIV)

You too, be patient and stand firm, because the Lord's coming is near. (James 5:8, NIV)

TEACHING OUR CHILDREN TO STAND

In order to stand, a person must have faith, which is the ability to believe that God has told the truth. The movie *Simon Birch* tells a wonderful story about faith. Simon, the main character, was an unusually small boy born with a weak heart. He was not expected to survive infancy, but Simon surprised everyone and lived. Simon firmly believed that God had given him life for a reason, a purpose that only he could fulfill. As the story unfolds, Simon searches until he finally discovers his destiny.

But the odds are against Simon. Not only is he small in stature and physically deformed, but his parents and most of society have no use for him. Throughout the movie Simon is taunted and teased by his peers and by adults. Everyone from his pastor to his best friend warns him to stop believing in his fantasy of a divine purpose. But Simon remains convinced. He can't explain *how* he knows that God has a plan for his life—he just knows it. He is convinced that he's an instrument of God.

Simon's faith eventually leads him to the fulfillment of his life purpose. And everyone realizes that Simon had a God-given purpose that he fulfilled in a unique way.

At one point Simon says, "I don't need proof [of God's plan]. I have faith." Faith is something with which we are born. Scripture does not tell us to find or create our faith but rather to build our faith (see Luke 17:5). We build on something that we already possess. Like a living thing, faith is something that we nurture, and then it grows. If we neglect faith, it withers and dies. Sadly, circumstances can tear down childlike faith before it has the opportunity to flourish.

How does faith grow? Faith develops as we put our trust in an authority who demonstrates reliability and consistency. That is why children believe in Santa Claus and the Easter Bunny. Parents tell their children stories about such characters, and since youngsters view their parents as reliable authorities, they believe them. Parents may also teach them that Jesus loves them, died for them, and will never forsake them. But as they grow and mature, they learn that there is no Santa, no Easter Bunny, and no fairy godmother. Then they begin to feel as if their parents have deceived them. And if Santa is a fairy tale, maybe Jesus is too. So they begin to challenge Jesus' existence—is he a real historical figure or just a fictional character?

Faith is knowing, believing, and standing on the truth even when circumstances or feelings suggest otherwise. Knowing is different than wondering. The foundation of spiritual warfare is knowing the truth. Thus we need to teach our children the truth, which the Bible and then God confirms through the Holy Spirit. If the Bible says it, they can believe in faith that it is true. And if it is true, they can stand on it—regardless of their circumstances or feelings. When we teach our children to use the Bible as God intended, that brings healing, hope, encouragement, and trust as the Holy Spirit comforts, teaches, and guides them.

If they do not believe the Bible to be true, they are perhaps not born again and will live in an ongoing cycle of defeat. If they have doubts about the Bible, they will be unable to press on in the midst of spiritual warfare. Accepting Jesus as their Savior is predicated on the knowledge that God's Word is true, that Jesus died for them, that he has forgiven them, and that he has a plan for them. Without faith in these realities, they cannot believe. And if they do not believe, it is because they do not trust that what God has said is true.

Belief + Trust = Faith

We must teach our children to have faith like Simon Birch, believing that God has a plan of spiritual success for their lives—a plan that includes living a life of freedom. That plan is available in a simple, understandable blueprint called the Bible. If they can learn to stand in faith on what the Bible says, then despite what their flesh and the world might say, great things are possible for them.

Faith heals, motivates, and cleanses. It moves mountains, breaks chains of demonic captivity, provides for our every need, and—most important—gives us eternal life. Faith is something that my eldest grandson, Jonathan, exercises whenever he stands on the couch while I encourage him to jump into my arms. I step back, open my arms wide, and say, "Okay, Jonathan, jump into Grammy's arms!" He reacts immediately, knowing that I will catch him just as I have always done. He bends his little knees, extends his arms, and springs off the couch into my arms with a trail of laughter following him. In the same way, we must encourage our children to put their faith into action because we know that God is able and willing to catch them when they jump into life's difficulties.

Putting faith into action is not easy for many children. When I was growing up, I would have hesitated to jump because there were times when *no one* was there to catch me. My father played emotional mind games with me that led to mistrust. He would catch me only *sometimes*. He would then tell me that the bumps and bruises, cuts and scars would make me stronger and self-reliant and that I could depend on no one but myself. His "lessons" bred doubt, insecurity, and a lack of faith. But God doesn't play such games. With arms open wide he promises, "I am here, waiting for you. It is safe to jump into my arms. I will not let you fall. I promise. I give you my word."

Smith Wigglesworth once said:

> God wants to sweep all unbelief from your heart. He wants you to dare to believe his Word. It is the Word of the Spirit. If you allow anything to come between you and the Word, it will poison your whole system, and you will have no hope. One bit of unbelief against the Word is poison. It is like the Devil putting a spear into you. The Word of Life is the breath of heaven, the life-giving power by which your very self is changed. By it, you begin to bear the image of the heavenly one.[30]

The enemy has disabled many children with his spear of unbelief because of early trauma they've experienced. We will find the power to heal that injury in our child's heart in God's Word. Will we begin to use its magnificent power and teach them to do the same? Or will we allow them to remain disabled, hopeless, and ineffective? We must discover and pass on to our children the truth that faith is "the substance of things hoped for, the evidence of things not seen" (Hebrews 11:1, NKJV). Things that we hope for in our children's lives and have not yet seen are visions for the future. The invisible is more real, or at least more lasting, than the visible. Faith is the foundation of all things in Christ, including spiritual warfare. We must not let life's circumstances shipwreck our children's faith. We can teach them to trust, to believe, and to walk in faith by our own example and by our teachings. Let us ask the Lord this very moment to increase our children's faith, remembering that "faith comes by hearing, and hearing by the word of God" (Romans 10:17, NKJV).

EXAMPLES OF THE COGNITIVE PROCESS

An examination of positive and negative examples of the cognitive process will help us recognize the underlying reasons for our own defeat or success (and our children's) in the spirit realm. We will use an example that is common to children—name-calling. Let's say Suzy is eight, in second grade, and comes home day after day crying because kids are calling her names. When you ask your daughter what's wrong, she tells you, "A boy at school, Tommy, keeps calling me a bucktoothed beaver." That's the event.

What might Suzy be thinking when he calls her names? You ask her, and she tells you, "I'm ugly! Nobody likes me! I don't have any friends!"

Even though you can see how she feels, you need to mirror what you are seeing. "Suzy, you look angry." More than likely she'll agree or tell you another feeling she's experiencing. Making a "feeling chart" that describes the basic feelings with facial expressions is a wonderful tool for children to use to identify their emotions.

Then ask her what she did when Tommy called her names. She

may tell you she ran away, told a teacher, or perhaps called him a name back. She may have done all those things, and add to the list, she's crying.

As a parent, how might we teach Suzy in this circumstance? How can we encourage her to combat the lies?

First, because something is assaulting her identity, we can identify this as a spiritual attack and can begin praying immediately against the lies that are assaulting her. Next, we can talk to her about what she knows God's Word says about her to combat the lies she's been told.

One of her thoughts is that she's ugly, but God's Word says that she is fearfully and wonderfully made, so that cannot be true. You could also tell her the beautiful, unique things that are evident in her as God created her. She's been told nobody likes her, but God's Word says that he loves her so much that he gave his only begotten Son for her sins. God's Word tells us that Jesus is a friend who sticks closer than a brother (Proverbs 18:24). You can also point out other friends and family you know who love her and other friends she has and plays with.

The reality of what she says or believes to be true is not the issue; so it makes no sense to try to reason with her. Furthermore, children do not learn thorough reasoning skills until they are approximately twelve years of age. So it's up to us as parents to teach our children appropriate ways to ward off lies.

EVENT: A BOY AT SCHOOL, TOMMY, KEEPS CALLING ME A BUCKTOOTHED BEAVER.

UNPLEASANT	PLEASANT
Thought:	*Thought:*
I'm ugly.	I am fearfully and wonderfully made.
I don't have any friends.	Jesus is my friend/closer than a brother.
Feelings:	*Feelings:*
Angry, rejected, unloved.	Safe, sure of self, confident.
Response:	*Response:*
Ran away and told teacher.	Tell teacher and parent for support.
Called him a name back.	Pray, standing in identity in Christ.
Came home crying.	Remain confident of self.

Can you see the difference in the potential outcome based on the different thought processes? In the fleshly example, what core belief might lead your child to believe that she is ugly and unwanted by friends? In this same situation, most parents, if the circumstance continues, would talk to the teacher and the child's parent. That is one aspect of the problem. We must also remember that we fight not against flesh and blood but against principalities; so we must also address this from a spiritual standpoint. Teaching our children how to take negative thoughts captive to Christ and look at the circumstance through God's eyes, with compassion, understanding, mercy, and love for self and others, is teaching them how to stand in truth.

There's another crucial element to this process. Your child may follow this process, taking every thought captive, experiencing healthy emotions, and responding in a godly way, and yet not experience the outcome that either of you desire. In the example listed above, the child who's calling your daughter names has a *will* that plays into this event. God did not make us to be robots. He set the biblical standard and commanded all of us to follow it. But we choose whether or not to submit our will to his will. While we may do extensive warfare on behalf of our child, the other child has a choice as well—either to rebel against the enemy spirit that is encouraging his behavior or to the Holy Spirit who is wooing him. In a perfect world we would want the verbally abusive child to ask for forgiveness, repent, and seek reconciliation with our child, but unfortunately, not all parents encourage this in child development. When the opportunity exists for two children to work through all steps to reconciliation, we should encourage it. Otherwise, children learn to run from hard situations. That is one of the major problems in marriages today. A lot of adults don't know how to push through the opposition, so they just give up.

The Bible is all about relationships: a relationship between God's people and himself, between mates and family, between believers and unbelievers. But relationships are difficult because they require a never-ending process of dying to self and submitting to God.

In Scripture we find other examples of both the fleshly process and the godly process, beginning with Satan, who was originally a perfect, anointed cherub (see Ezekiel 28:12-13). He gazed upon God's glory, desired to be like him, attempted to take what he wanted, and became the enemy of God.

Eve was the perfect creation of God but was enticed by forbidden fruit and her desire to be like God. She took the fruit for herself and gave it to Adam, who with Eve ushered sin into the world and earned expulsion from the Garden of Eden.

David, the second king of Israel, fell spiritually when he saw Bathsheba and desired her for himself even though she was the wife of another man. David took her for himself, lied and created a web of deception, and caused the death of Bathsheba's husband, Uriah. The result was a break in David's fellowship with God, the death of his son, and a legacy of sorrow in his family line.

There is something else that we must consider: we must not expect that just because children choose to take their thoughts captive, they will be exempt from heartache or pain. If their parents divorce, the children will experience the agony of a broken covenant. If someone close to children dies, they will grieve. When someone lies or gossips about them, that will hurt their feelings. However, by continually taking their thoughts captive, they will, with the help of the Holy Spirit, be able to hold their emotions in check. Then they will learn to go to their knees in prayer and fight the battle that is at hand.

There are also other spiritual techniques that we can use to battle against the principalities and spiritual forces that attack our children. First and foremost, however, we must understand that we can do everything perfectly and still not see the outcome that we desire. Always remember that in spiritual battle someone else's will is often involved.

9

FAITH AND COMMUNICATION WITH GOD

He who dwells in the shelter of the Most High
will abide in the shadow of the Almighty.

PSALM 91:1

"What's the difference between prayer, intercession, and spiritual warfare?" The question came from a father in Budapest, Hungary, where I was teaching spiritual warfare to missionary parents and their children. "Aren't they all the same?" he added curiously. The answer is yes, but no. Some similarities between the three include that they are all an outpouring of the heart, verbal communication with God, and acts of faith. Equally so, they breed spiritual trust and belief in God. But when you get into specifics, you'll find that although they are interchangeable types of communication, they are different in purpose.

Prayer is doxology—that is, communication with God that includes thanksgiving, confession, and supplication. When we pray, we have direct contact with God and generally address our sinful behavior, our needs, and gratefulness for his provision. Scripture admonishes us to devote ourselves to prayer, to pray at all times, and not to cease praying (Colossians 4:2; Ephesians 6:18; 1 Thessalonians 5:17).

The purpose of prayer is to develop intimacy and trust with God, our Heavenly Father. Through prayer we gain spiritual strength, are equipped to resist temptation, receive wisdom when asking for it, and develop intimacy through being in God's presence. When we pray, we are in instant communication with our Creator. Unlike a doctor's office, we do not have to listen to elevator music and read last year's *Good Housekeeping* while we wait our turn to see him. During our prayerful conversation with God, we may also pray for others, and when we do so, that is called intercession.

An intercessor is best described as a person who is an advocate of another person—that is, someone who stands in the gap for another person's best interest. As parents, we intercede or stand in the gap for our children. Intercession is different from prayer in that while we can advocate for their behalf as we do our own, we cannot confess our children's sins or receive Christ for them. When we petition God for our children's needs, we do so in accordance with his will. We know God's will based on what he has said in his Word, the Bible.

A parent intercessor is similar to what the legal courts refer to as a *Guardian ad litem*. A guardian is generally appointed by a judge to know a child's specific needs and to advocate for what is best for the child. In the event of abuse or even a divorce at times, a *Guardian ad litem* will spend time with the child and with other pertinent people involved in the child's life, will make a plea to the courts based on his or her findings, and will make a recommendation on the child's behalf. The one question every *Guardian ad litem* must answer for the judge is: what is best for this child? The judge reviews the information given by the guardian in relation to the case and makes a decision.

Jesus is the ultimate intercessor or *Guardian ad litem* for us as described in Isaiah 53:12: "he bore the sin of many, and makes intercession for the transgressors." He interceded for us before the Judge, God himself, for our best interest. That is, he paid the price of our sin so that we could enjoy intimate fellowship with our Heavenly Father. In addition, because of our frailty as humans, our Creator gave us another intercessor, the Holy Spirit, who prays for our best interest in accordance with God's will (Romans 8:26-27). Our Father in heaven is so faithful a parent that he models the behavior he expects from his spiritual children, just as we parents should for our earthly children. Thus he tells us that we too are to be intercessors, "that we may live peaceful and quiet lives in all godliness and holiness" (1 Timothy 2:2, NIV).

Spiritual warfare involves both prayer and intercession but is more spiritually aggressive in nature because it involves a supernatural encounter in which God's power is accessed by the believer through faith. Unlike prayer and intercession, spiritual warfare involves using weapons in order to demolish strongholds, arguments, and any other pretension that sets itself against us (2 Corinthians 10:3-5) and also involves wearing or using the armor of God (Ephesians 6:10-18). Prayer and intercession typically do not include being both offensive and defensive in nature, but spiritual warfare tactically encompasses both aspects and involves man, God, spirits, angels, and childlike faith.

WHY WE FIGHT THE BATTLE

Communication is the main component of all three aspects of interaction with God—prayer, intercession, and spiritual warfare. And as we just learned, all three of those types of communication are void of power without faith. Generally when we seek communication with God, we begin with prayer, addressing our own deficiencies and needs. Next we petition, intercede, or advocate for others' needs. Are these types of prayer efficient communication with God? Yes. Are they effective? Absolutely. So why engage in spiritual warfare at all?

The reason we must engage in battle is because we have no other choice. If our country were brutally attacked by another one, we would have two choices: one, to defend ourselves and engage in protecting our land and rights, or, two, to stand in the destructive aftermath and do nothing. The problem with the latter choice is that choosing to do nothing is still a choice, and it does not change the fact that war has been engaged with us. I can reject the law of gravity as a belief, but it is still a part of everyday life for everyone. I can even make a decision to defy the law of gravity and attempt to live my life void of the law by jumping off a roof, but despite my defiance toward the law of gravity, because it remains in effect I will promptly and perhaps fatally harm myself.

Spiritual warfare is a spiritual fact. From the day we are born until the moment we die, we are in a spiritual battle, romanced by good and seduced by evil. We can stand idly by and watch our children fall by the wayside and become spiritual fatalities, or we can pick up our swords and fight on their behalf and teach them to do the same.

I had a woman tell me in a spiritual warfare conference that she didn't have the "personality" to be a warrior for her children. Her husband nodded in agreement, then added, "Yeah, it's not really our style."

I thought for a moment before I responded, then asked them, "What would you do if you took your children to the park one day and while your child was playing, someone came up and started hitting, kicking, and yelling at your child?" Horror and rage flashed across the mother's face, and the father sat up defensively in his chair.

"I'd intervene! I'd do whatever it took to stop the assailant from doing that!" he said matter-of-factly. His wife nodded her head in agreement, then added, "I'd never let anyone treat my child that way!"

"That's right," I said. "I wouldn't let that happen to my child either. You *are* a warrior, a fighter." I looked at the father, then the mother. "You'd be like two lions who are defending their cub from an intruder. Satan is a perpetrator. His desire is to destroy your child's faith. In doing so, he will assault your child from every possible avenue. What are you willing to do about that?"

It is inevitable that the time will come when your children will be absent from you and will need to access the heavenlies on their own. So it's equally as important for us to teach them the difference between different types of communication and when to apply them. A spiritual attack is potentially more damaging, having lifelong effects, than any physical attack we could endure. This is because spiritual warfare involves our intellect, our emotions, our core beliefs about ourselves and the world around us, and our beliefs about God.

Satan's war tactics are subtle but methodical. Like that of many of the historical commanders in earthly armies of the past, Satan's objective is to disrupt communication among the opposing troops. If an army succeeds in interrupting the communication between the opposing commander and his soldiers, that army will win. As believers we have a direct line of contact with our Commander twenty-four hours a day, seven days a week. Spiritual warfare is more than just a dialogue between believers and God; it is an avenue that brings intimacy into the relationship and unleashes the power of God himself. It involves give and take and our learning to be honest and transparent with an all-knowing God and joining him in his will.

Scripture tells us to pray without ceasing (1 Thessalonians 5:17). Many have made prayer a ritual by getting on their knees, folding their palms together, bowing their heads, and closing their eyes. Though these practices do promote reverence, consistency, and honor to God, this is not the only way to encourage our children to pray. They can pray to God while standing, with eyes open, with hands raised, whispering, or talking out loud. They can honor their Heavenly Father while they are sitting in school, cleaning their rooms, or doing their homework. He is with them always. They should feel the freedom to talk to him, praise him, sing to him, thank him, and confess their sins to him at all times. Whatever we do, we should teach them to never stop communicating with their Heavenly Father.

Hymn-writer James Montgomery said, "Prayer is the soul's sincere desire, uttered or unexpressed; the motion of a hidden fire that trembles in the breast." Montgomery describes a passion that burns deep inside *each* Christ-follower—even children! The greatest, most powerful prayer warriors that I know are under the age of eighteen, and most of them are less than four feet tall!

Whenever communication stops between God and our children, they will become confused, lost, and spiritually discouraged until it resumes. When we notice our children becoming distant and withdrawn, confused or discouraged, we must encourage them to talk about it not only to us but to their Heavenly Father. Doing so will heal their hearts, not to mention ours. If our children choose not to engage in communication with him again, they will begin to doubt, to question, and to resist what they know is right and will allow the world to start shaping them. They cannot serve two masters. One of two persons will always be shaping our children's spiritual development—God or Satan.

One of the most vital aspects of communication is listening. Some people say they don't "hear" God speak to them, and if they can't hear God's voice, how can they teach their children to do so? Jesus said, "My sheep listen to my voice" (John 10:27, NIV). The issue isn't that we are *unable* to hear God's voice; we simply fail to *listen* for it. Either that or we question it when we hear it because we aren't used to listening! Another glaring problem in hearing God's voice is lack of faith—that is, doubting when we've heard from God.

There are ways to assure that the voice we're hearing is our Father's and not our own or the enemy's. First of all, God's direction for us in our lives is never contrary to what he says in the Bible. In other words, he would not direct someone to gossip or slander when he clearly states that's wrong. Second, our Father is consistent and is a God of character; thus he would never lead us to act or respond to a situation in a way that is contrary to the characteristics he himself possesses—integrity, patience, love, peace, joy, and more.

When we seek God's counsel, he will reward us diligently by giving us precise instruction on how to respond in any given situation. But we must often seek his Word and character, talk to him in prayer, and ask for direction. We also have to be willing to spend whatever time it takes to hear his voice as we pursue his presence.

Prayer is communication with God, a way to claim his promises and to receive his blessings, guidance, and wisdom. One of the greatest things about prayer is that he promises to respond to us, to hear the prayers of the sinner who seeks forgiveness, and to act on the request of everyone who asks in Jesus' name (see John 14:13-14). God even answers prayers when we can't find the right words to say. And he always does more than we ask (Ephesians 3:20).

Some say they don't pray because God already knows their hearts, so why tell him? But it is not enough for God to know our hearts. Do we not want to know his? Prayer is the only way that change will occur in our lives. It is to be an intimate communication between the Creator and his creatures. It would be just as silly for our children to say, "Why communicate with my parents when they know how I feel?" You wouldn't accept that statement, and neither does God. Many believers have needs that go unmet simply because they do not pray (see James 4:2).

Prayer is also an expression of dependence upon God and humility. When our children go to him with their concerns, they are saying, "I know I cannot make it through this day and live according to your will without you. I need you. I need your Spirit to guide me." This dependence is at the core of spiritual warfare. In battle we must encourage our children to cling to nothing more than they do to God. That's it—period. Victory in spiritual warfare requires utter dependence on God, his will, and his Word. Our prayers as parents must be in agreement with what God has done in the past, what he is doing at the present, and what he promises to do in our children's future. We know what our children's future holds because it's outlined in God's Word.

Prayer is our direct line to our Commander. Through prayer God offers direction and encouragement. Furthermore, our prayers are "powerful and effective" (see James 5:16, NIV). Consider two biblical characters whom Satan brutally attacked—Job and Nehemiah. Both were attacked—directly and indirectly—by the Devil, whose purpose was to undermine God's work. Satan often uses other people to attack believers.

The enemies of Nehemiah ridiculed him, mocked him, and conspired to attack him. And how did Nehemiah respond? By praying in each and every instance of spiritual attack. Nehemiah never took action without first consulting God in prayer.

The same was true of Job. Satan accused Job before God and robbed him of his health, his wealth, and his children. Job's wife ridiculed him and encouraged him to curse God. His friends unjustly accused him of sin. Job's response? He prayed and praised God, trusting in his Redeemer and proclaiming God's righteousness.

In response to the prayers of both men, God was faithful and blessed them. One of the key ingredients that empowered their prayers was their willing submission to God. Scripture tells us that believers must submit themselves to God and resist the Devil, and then the enemy will flee (James 4:7). Our children learn to submit to God by being obedient, putting on the full armor of God as he commands. It is then that they are able to resist the Devil. And when they pray with God's power, Satan *will* flee. Guaranteed.

COMMUNICATION ROADBLOCKS IN OUR WARFARE

Several factors are self-imposed roadblocks to communication between believers and God. Here are just a few:

• Believers would rather ignore the obvious and live in defeat than exert the energy needed to be spiritually combative. Like an ostrich, they think that if they keep their head buried in the sand, they'll be exempt from pain or difficulties.

• Believers are preoccupied with other things—bills, appointments, frustrations, work, etc. Whatever we don't give over to God is bound to taunt us. We must go to him and lay all things before him if we want to clear our minds so we can hear his voice.

• Believers are afraid to be spiritually aggressive, fearing they'll turn into "holy rollers."

• Believers don't feel they have the necessary vocabulary to talk to God.

• Believers have their own agendas, expectations, and will apart from God's.

• Believers have unresolved anger or negative beliefs about God.

• Believers allow outside interference or distractions.

• Time pressures do not allow effective communication to occur.

Many other factors can also steal opportunities for us to seek God and his will, but we should go to whatever extreme is necessary to assure that our communication with God is not hindered, because without it we are like a ship without a rudder.

THE POWER OF
WORDS

Fathers, do not provoke your children to anger, but bring
them up in the discipline and instruction of the Lord.

EPHESIANS 6:4

Parents have immense biblical authority to influence the destiny of
their children for better or for worse. Their words are not mere
words—they carry with them the power to bless or curse. I always
encourage parents to be extra-concerned and careful about what they
speak over their children because, first, children hang on every word
we say and take it personally, and, second, we will be held accountable for every word we speak.

It is said that it takes thirteen positive words to eliminate one negative one from one's mind. Oh, that we could grasp the full understanding
of the power of our words! The Bible is not silent on the use of this power.

> *There is one whose rash words are like sword thrusts,*
> *but the tongue of the wise brings healing.*

PROVERBS 12:18

> *The tongue that brings healing is a tree of life,*
> *but a deceitful tongue crushes the spirit.*

PROVERBS 15:4, NIV

Gracious words are like a honeycomb.

PROVERBS 16:24

Whoever keeps his mouth and his tongue
keeps himself out of trouble.

PROVERBS 21:23

The tongue, though small, has enormous influence. Like a river, the words that flow from our mouths carve out a path in our children's hearts. At times that path can be like a gentle and pleasant stream that runs through a backyard and leads them on a course of success in life. At other times it floods their hearts and destroys everything it touches, including their identity, esteem, and faith.

Matthew 12:34 tells us that, just as a river has its source, so do our words. They flow from the heart: "For out of the abundance of the heart the mouth speaks." Romans 10:9-10 even tells us, "if you confess with your mouth that Jesus is Lord and believe in your heart that God raised him from the dead, you will be saved. For with the heart one believes and is justified, and with the mouth one confesses and is saved."

What our hearts believe, our mouths speak, and the same is true for our children, thus revealing another way to access what our children hold onto as their core beliefs. Once we identify what those beliefs are, we can examine them to see if they are in agreement with God's Word. And once we do that, we can encourage our children to speak the truth and expect the biblical result to manifest itself.

THE WEIGHT OF A WORD

The power of God's word was evident even before the earth began. John 1:1 says, "In the beginning was the Word, and the Word was with God, and the Word was God." And in Genesis 1 we read, "And God said, 'Let there be light,' and there was light. . . . And God said, 'Let there be an expanse in the midst of the waters, and let it separate the waters from the waters.' . . . And it was so" (1:3, 6-7). The creation of the world came about through God's spoken word. So words in line with God's Word are also powerful.

This is an important aspect of spiritual warfare because we can create an atmosphere of defeat for our children with negative or ungodly talk about them and to them. Parents must claim the freedom in Christ for their children that God promises through Christ. This is not some name-it-and-claim-it theology. Rather, it is believing that what God's Word says is true and then speaking it, just as Romans 10:9-10 says to do. This type of verbal faith in action has the power to lead our children to salvation and to empower them to overcome trials, resist temptations, and tear down strongholds. It also produces fruit in the lives of people around them.

Valarie, a friend of mine and a single parent, was going through great difficulty with her eldest child, Jon. Her son had been ensnared in the web of drugs for approximately five years, and she was confident he was selling them as well. Jon's father had abandoned him and his mother when he was only five. While Jon remembers little about his interactions with his father, he remembered clearly his words telling him he'd never amount to anything but drugs and jail. While his words were not the ultimate reason Jon's life led to such a lifestyle, they tore down any hope within the child that he'd ever become anything more.

Valarie noticed several of her expensive household items such as her DVD player and television starting to disappear under the guise of being "borrowed" or "stolen." She suspected Jon was selling them to get money for drugs. She wanted to storm the gates of hell so her son would be delivered, but she found herself immobilized by her pain and love as a parent. In her spiritually weak state she would pray, "Lord, I pray that if it's your will, my son will be delivered from drugs and you will protect my belongings in my house. In Jesus' name, Amen."

Is there anything wrong with that prayer? Yes. Defeat is written all over it. It is covered with doubt and disbelief. Is it God's will to deliver her son from drugs? Absolutely. Is it God's will to protect her personal items? Certainly. It *is* God's will that Valarie not be afraid of her son, that he be delivered and walk in freedom, and that her household items not be stolen. A more powerful prayer would involve faith (belief + trust) that what God's Word says is true:

Lord, your Word says that you desire that all would come to the saving knowledge of Jesus Christ. Therefore, I pray for Jon's salvation in the name of Jesus. I pray that you will intervene and do whatever it takes to get my son's attention so that he will turn from the lies of the enemy and the web of deceit by which drugs have ensnared him. I stand against Satan and his cohorts and the lies he is whispering to my son, in the name of Jesus. O God, please command Satan to release his hold on my son *now*, in Jesus' name. Father, stand against the Adversary on my behalf. You have said that you are for me, and thus no one can be against me, and I thank you for that. I thank you that you have placed a hedge of protection around me and my home. I thank you that you have called me your own and have said that I and my household will be saved. You sent your son Jesus to set Jon free, and I receive that promise in Jon's life as his parent. I pray that he would accept the freedom that you offer him in the name of Jesus. You also say in Jonah 3:8 that it's your will that man give up his evil ways. Lord, I know that it's your will that my son be delivered from this. So I pray that he will miraculously align his will with yours. It was you who softened the heart of Pharaoh for a time, allowing Moses and your people to walk away in freedom. I accept that same blessing in my son's life. It is in the power that raised Jesus Christ from the dead that I pray. Amen.

That prayer is one of power because it is from the Word of God, and it was the Word of God that brought the universe into existence. It was the Word of God that raised Jesus from the dead, and it will be the Word of God that sets your child free from the strongholds and attacks of the enemy.

Valarie began to pray, believing that God would do the work that he spoke of in his Word. As she began to pray in faith, Jon's heart softened. He began attending a youth group after he got arrested for possession of drugs. He also was required to attend some twelve-step groups that helped him get on track. As part of his punishment, Jon was required to go to counseling with his mother, and together they were able to work through some pretty tough issues. Today Jon is a godly young man in college studying to become a drug and alcohol counselor. God has used what Satan had intended for evil for his glory (Romans 8:28). I look forward to seeing what God does with Jon in the future.

GOD'S WILL AND OUR CHILDREN'S WILL

Another issue is the will—God's will, our will, and the will of our children. Knowing God's will and following it requires prayer and a commitment to studying and obeying his Word. But there is a factor other than our will that comes into play. Even if we know God's will and are walking in it, we must also consider the will of our children.

God did not make us robots; instead he gave us free will. We make our own choices, making decisions and living with the consequences. The decisions of other people also affect us. Vast numbers of people are in counseling because of sexual and physical abuse, lack of esteem due to verbal abuse, or a parent's addiction. All of these and more are a result of someone else's sin. God will soften someone's heart, but he will not make up a person's mind for him or her. The choices are ours, and ours alone.

Now, many parents have prayed the same powerful prayer as Valarie did, but their sons did not change. Instead their children went further into sin. Some of them haven't returned to this day. This is not to say that God is through with them, and they still may turn their hearts back to him. I mention this because I want to emphasize that this did not happen because the parents didn't pray hard enough or long enough. It is because their children's will has yet to be aligned with God's. Our job is not to decide whether or not the other person is going to change or to convict someone of sin or make them change. Our responsibility is to pray God's Word and to rely on him to lead us in our prayers. If we are seeking God's will, he will reveal to us what step to take next and when to take it when praying for our children.

As we pray God's will, the faith factor is crucial. We must believe that what we are saying is true. If we don't believe, we need to confess that to the Lord as sin and ask him to build up faith in our hearts. We must cover ourselves with his Word.

THE AUTHORITATIVE WORD

In October 2002 I received an invitation to the White House to attend the Missing, Exploited, and Runaway Children's Conference hosted by President George W. Bush and First Lady Laura Bush. I had the pleasure of meeting the President and talking with him briefly about his faith in God. I will never forget the words that this godly man spoke. When he speaks, he does so with great power and authority. When President Bush gives orders, those who are under his command carry out his wishes without hesitation. But as much power as the President's words have, their power is nothing in comparison to the power of God's words in the lives of those who trust in and live by those words.

To what degree are God's words authoritative in our lives? When God says something, do we question it, or do we walk in it without hesitation? Do we bathe ourselves and our children in the truths that he has spoken, or do we dismiss them? We ought always to claim God's words as truth, speak them out, and walk obediently in them as the standard for our own children.

Knowledge of the power of God's Word is vital for both parents and their children because it is his Word that enables us to walk in freedom. Just verbally speaking out the Word of God involves faith. There are promises in God's Word for the parent who calls out to him, and his promise is deliverance: "In the day of my trouble I call upon you, for you answer me" (Psalm 86:7). "Call to Me, and I will answer you, and show you great and mighty things, which you do not know" (Jeremiah 33:3, NKJV).

There will be times when we will not know how or what we should pray for our children. At such a time it is sufficient to come into God's presence on our faces, weeping and confused, knowing that Jesus is at the right hand of God interceding for us. Our words have the power to heal or destroy. God's Word, when we obey it, live by it, and speak it out boldly, has the power to defeat every foe. Our words, when they are God's words, are powerful indeed. And when we speak them in the power and conviction of the Holy Spirit, relying on him, we are invincible.

FLANKING OUR CHILDREN IN THE ARMOR OF GOD

Prepare buckler and shield,
and advance for battle!
Harness the horses;
mount, O horsemen!
Take your stations with your helmets,
polish your spears,
put on your armor!

JEREMIAH 46:3-4

Once your children have come to the saving knowledge of Jesus Christ, they automatically inherit God's blessings and enemies. Knowing this would occur, their Heavenly Father has given them the gift of armor to "stand against the schemes of the devil" (Ephesians 6:11). Each piece is distinctive and unique, but our children must know the significance of each and must put on each piece if they are to overcome the attacks of Satan.

As a parent, you can help your children dress in the armor, but you cannot put it on them yourself. This is because when putting the armor on, a moral inventory of each piece must be done. For example, "the belt of truth" cannot be placed on one's waist without considering where, since your last application of the belt, you have been less than truthful. The one dressing himself or herself must repent of those falsehoods and protect himself or herself with the belt. Truth cannot be just laid over falsehood. The falsehood must be removed first. Because we cannot repent for another person, we can only pray for and remind our children to do this themselves and assist them when and where necessary.

The most instrumental thing we can do in conjunction to this, then, is to educate our children on the command of God's Word to protect oneself—that is, the significance of each part of the armor and how to use it offensively or defensively according to his Word.

In Ephesians 6 the apostle Paul writes about how to be strong in the midst of opposition by putting on God's armor. Consider verses 10-20:

> Finally, be strong in the Lord and in the strength of his might. Put on the whole armor of God, that you may be able to stand against the schemes of the devil. For we do not wrestle against flesh and blood, but against the rulers, against the authorities, against the cosmic powers over this present darkness, against the spiritual forces of evil in the heavenly places. Therefore take up the whole armor of God, that you may be able to withstand in the evil day, and having done all, to stand firm. Stand therefore, having fastened on the belt of truth, and having put on the breastplate of righteousness, and, as shoes for your feet, having put on the readiness given by the gospel of peace. In all circumstances take up the shield of faith, with which you can extinguish all the flaming darts of the evil one; and take the helmet of salvation, and the sword of the Spirit, which is the word of God, praying at all times in the Spirit, with all prayer and supplication. To that end keep alert with all perseverance, making supplication for all the saints, and also for me, that words may be given to me in opening my mouth boldly to proclaim the mystery of the gospel, for which I am an ambassador in chains, that I may declare it boldly, as I ought to speak.

Paul tells the aspiring soldier to "be strong in the Lord and in the strength of his might." Your children must draw all the resources they need from Christ and his power. The Greek word for Christ's power here is *kratos*, the same word for the power that raised Jesus from the dead and the same power that brought us to life in Christ when we were dead in trespasses and sins. It means "to take hold of, grasp, have power over, hold in one's hand." It is a proclamation that we are not alone, that Christ is not only with us, but we have the power of Christ at hand. We can, therefore, be strong in his power, knowing that we do not fight the battle alone.

THE ARMOR THAT ASSURES VICTORY

Paul also told believers to "put on the whole armor of God, that you may be able to stand against the schemes of the devil." One of the most wonderful things about the spiritual armor is that the Bible describes God wearing the very same armaments. Isaiah 11:5 tells us that righteousness is God's belt and faithfulness is the sash around his waist. Isaiah 59:17 tells us that righteousness is also his breastplate, that he wears the helmet of salvation on his head, and that he wears the garments of vengeance and wraps himself in zeal as his cloak. What an honor it is to help dress our children in armor similar to that of their Commander! And what child doesn't like to play "dress up"? The armor is one of my favorite things to teach children.

Because our Creator knew every part of our bodies inside and out, including our strengths and weaknesses, he designed a covering that would shield every part of our bodies, from head to foot.

The items of the armor appear in the order in which they should be put on as your children prepare for battle. Once the armor is on, it leaves no place on their body or their life uncovered.

First, they are to gird their waists with truth (see Ephesians 6:14). It is the same belt of truth that the Messiah wears in Isaiah 11:5. "Truth" in this verse represents both the truth of the gospel and the truth within us. In biblical battles the belt was crucial because it kept the breastplate in place. When we consider that the belt (truth) holds up the breastplate (righteousness), it becomes obvious how the different pieces of the armor work in conjunction and build upon each other. Additionally, the sword hung from the belt and needed to be held securely for easy retrieval. When the warrior wore his belt, he was prepared for action. He loosened it only when he was off duty.

In Bible times, the waist or abdominal area represented the seat of emotions. To gird this area with truth is to commit your emotions to believing the truth. Children of the King must hold a commitment to truth regardless of the repercussions. Standing for truth often hurts other people's feelings. That can sometimes be heart-wrenching, but when there is a choice between pleasing the world or pleasing God, our children's choice must always be to please their Heavenly Father.

As I mentioned earlier, the belt of truth cannot be applied without considering where, since the last application of the armor, one has been less than honest. Since "truth" represents both the truth of the gospel and the truth within us, both need to be considered. When doing this moral inventory, we must consider where we may have accepted lies from the enemy or others in regard to God and his Word, as well as where we have stretched the truth, lied by omission, or told a barefaced lie, or even little white lies. You can see the wonderful teaching opportunities you will have with your child as you discuss all the possibilities of dishonesty.

Second, believers are to put on "the breastplate of righteousness" (Ephesians 6:14). The breastplate covered a soldier's body from the neck to the thighs and covered both the front and back of the soldier. "Righteousness" represents integrity of character.

When our children wear the breastplate of righteousness, they deal fairly with others because they are using a biblical standard. In short, they play fair with others, and their behavior matches their spiritual beliefs and words. As we encourage our children to wear the breastplate of righteousness, we are building integrity and character into their lives. Just as they did with the belt of truth, they must consider where they have not been righteous in their behavior, which inadvertently encourages a moral inventory of behavior that leads to repentance.

One of the greatest aspects of the armor is that it teaches our children conviction as opposed to condemnation as they do their own moral inventory. It teaches them how to repent, what areas to examine, and what is expected of them merely by the name of each piece. More adults could benefit by doing the same!

Once the breastplate has been fitted into position, our children must prepare their feet with "the gospel of peace" (Ephesians 6:15). In biblical history, preparing one's feet for war was vital because the terrain one would encounter was often uncertain. It was the one piece of armor that a soldier could not go without because if his feet were not shod he was limited in his mobility.

The military success of Alexander the Great is said to be, in large part, the result of his army being well shod and able to make long marches at incredible speed over rough terrain. In the same way, when believers are about their Father's business, ready to go anyplace to spread the gospel of peace and reconciliation, they need to prepare their feet for the journey. As noted in the first chapter, parents are often deficient in teaching their children how to shoe their feet with the gospel of Jesus Christ. As equally noted, this is because we as parents are often not well shod ourselves. Thus, this is an area we can learn about alongside our children.

Believers are commanded to spread the gospel (Mark 16:15). So shoeing our children's feet includes repenting for lost opportunities, times we were silent when we could have shared, for not taking the necessary time to learn how to properly shoe our feet, and more.

In addition, the believer is to "take up the shield of faith" (Ephesians 6:16). The shield of the Roman soldier was generally large and oblong. It consisted of two layers of wood glued together, covered with linen and hide, which they would saturate with water and bind with iron. A soldier's shield provided excellent protection, especially when he fought side by side with his fellow soldiers, presenting to the enemy a solid wall of shields. This side-by-side battle technique occurs every time parents and children pray together.

In ancient warfare arrows or darts were often dipped in pitch and then ignited to serve as deadly incendiary weapons. The believer's shield of faith does not simply deflect such missiles but actually quenches the flames to prevent them from spreading. The fiery darts of the Wicked One are often doubt, fear, shame, guilt, and legalism, but the God of Truth enables us to stand and deflect them. God's Word, which is truth, enables us to stand against them (John 8:32).

When doing the moral inventory of this piece of armor, we will find ourselves encouraging our children to look for spiritual wounds. Where have the attacks of the world and Satan landed blows? Where have our children accepted doubt, fear, shame, guilt, or legalism into their hearts? When eliminating these wounds in our child's spirit, we must encourage them to renounce the acceptance of those assaults and verbally stand in receptivity of healing by accepting the opposite. For example, if they have received doubt, they must renounce and replace it with assurance of their acceptance in Christ.

Two more items remain: "the helmet of salvation" and "the sword of the Spirit" (see Ephesians 6:17). The soldier's helmet covered his head and was most commonly made of bronze, with leather attachments. Putting on the helmet of salvation protects the head and, in the spiritual sense, the mind. When our heads are not covered, any number of thoughts can assault our minds and lead us off course. I have seen many casualties of war in this area when it comes to the assurance of salvation. The Devil puts doubt and insecurity into the minds of believers, and because their heads are not covered with the helmet of salvation, they begin to wonder which side they belong to. This is what we today call brainwashing. If the enemy can get into the soldier's head and reprogram his thought processes, he can cause devastation.

Parents, we will someday be held responsible for what we've allowed our children to watch, participate in, and listen to. The majority of things on television and radio are direct assaults on our children's minds. Thus we must repent for what we've given our children permission to watch or listen to, and our children must repent for what things we've inadvertently allowed into their ear and eye gates.

The last piece of armor that we are told to put on is "the sword of the Spirit, which is the word of God" (see Ephesians 6:17). It is the only offensive weapon in the armor. Luke 4 tells us that when Jesus was combating Satan, he refuted the father of lies with the truth of God's Word (Matthew 4:4, 7, 10).

The Word of God is powerful, effective, instructive, and razor-sharp (see Hebrews 4:12; 2 Timothy 3:16-17). It is not *our* sword, but the sword of the Spirit of God who resides in us. The power we access within us when we use the Word of God in combat enables the bearer of the sword to fight the battle at hand with confidence, strength, and surety.

In a study conducted by George Barna, parents were asked what spiritual areas they thought were their children's weak areas. The two overwhelming answers were: knowing how to study the Bible and memorizing Bible verses. Warfare is impossible without these two elements. Left on their own accord, our children will be consumed, chewed up, and spit out by the enemy of their souls. Not teaching our children how to study the Bible and apply its principles is equivalent to not feeding them physically. We'd never dream of withholding food from a developing child, and yet that's exactly what we do spiritually if we don't give them the Word of God. As a matter of fact, the government would intervene in our children's lives if we failed to feed them food on a daily basis, and yet we starve their souls, the very nourishment they need most in life.

In doing a moral inventory with the sword of the Spirit, children must consider where, out of their own selfishness, they may have used God's Word out of context to feed their sinful nature. An example would be areas where they have pushed the envelope of sin without actually committing the offense itself. Compromising God's Word is a great offense of which we are all guilty. I am more likely to measure my sin against someone else's actions rather than with what the Bible says. In doing so, I may feel justified that I'm not as bad as another person, but I would be wrong. We must teach our children that although God's Word is convicting and humbles us, it also provides the balm of healing through Christ. This leads us to another area of confession regarding the sword of the Spirit—areas of our life where we have stood on the world's standard of restoration rather than on God's found in the Word. That is not to say that our Heavenly Father does not use tools found in the world such as physicians, medications, and so on, but we must first and foremost find the truth of healing in the Word and stand on it.

Basically, in examining our sin in regard to the sword of the Spirit, we must consider anywhere we have turned our back on the Holy

Spirit and the Word of God, the Bible. God is faithful to show us where we have turned away from him and his ways and have followed our own.

Finally, we are told to pray always (see Ephesians 6:18). Prayer opens the channels of communication between God and his children. In the midst of battle, God's children must stay in constant contact with their Leader for directions and encouragement. Our prayers for our children are important and effective (see James 5:16), and we must never believe the lie that God does not hear and answer our prayers. Further, we must teach our children how to converse with their Heavenly Father. One way we can do this is by having open, honest communication with them ourselves. Children often base their core beliefs about God's character on their relationship with their biological parents. If Mom or Dad are legalistic and show conditional love based on their children's behavior, it will take much work and conscious effort not to see God in that same light. Additionally, I encourage parents to stay away from standard prayers that can easily fall into routine communication—a chore. Instead, allow your children to hear you pray honestly and vulnerably about situations your family is going through. Let them see you petition God for his guidance, wisdom, and direction. Allow them to see you grappling with his truth but also submitting to it. Children are so impressionable and will remember what they see you demonstrate in your communication with God.

When we pray, God makes us alert to what is happening around us and in our children's lives through the Holy Spirit. When we pray, the Spirit of God teaches us, leads us, and reveals to us the strategies of the enemy and even the motives of our children. Amazingly, the Holy Spirit would tell me whenever my son, Paul, would lie to me. After finally confessing the truth he'd ask, "How do you always know when I'm lying?" I'd tell him that I don't know, but God does, and he gives me the discernment to know. That taught him that although I didn't see and hear everything, God did, and Paul had a higher authority to answer to than just Mom.

Without the righteousness of Christ, the truth, the gospel of peace, the shield of faith, the helmet of salvation, and the sword of the Spirit, our children will not be motivated to pray but instead will want to fulfill the desires of their flesh. Apart from the armor, our children become vulnerable to the enemy's taunting and as a result become more susceptible to sin.

Once our children are protected with the armor, they are to "stand against" the wiles of the enemy (Ephesians 6:11). The word translated "stand" is a military term that means "to hold one's position." The armor enables our children to ward off the attacks of the enemy and to take a stand against him. Before our children are able to launch any offensive, they must learn how to stand their own ground. The word "stand" is used four times in this passage, emphasizing the need for steadfastness in the face of our ruthless foe. The word "against" stresses the determined hostility that confronts the believer. The commander-in-chief of the opposing forces is the Devil himself. He is a master of ingenious strategies, and we must not allow him to catch our children unawares.

THE VALUE OF HEDGES AND ANGELS

In addition to his armor, God provides for the believer two other types of protection. The first is the hedge of God that the Devil complained about in Job 1:10: "Have you not put a hedge around him and his house and all that he has, on every side?" This hedge cannot be penetrated without God's permission, and it identifies which side of the battle we are on.

God also provides his angels, who continually minister to believers. "He will command his angels concerning you to guard you in all your ways" (Psalm 91:11). "Are they not all ministering spirits sent out to serve for the sake of those who are to inherit salvation?" (Hebrews 1:14).

We are told first to put on the full armor of God, that we may be able to stand firm against the enemy's attacks. God's hedge and God's angels are not our only means of protection. Scripture also admonishes us to stand and fight. God not only protects us—he also gives us detailed instructions on how to defend ourselves. He even provides specialized training for us.

According to the Foreign Military Studies office, infantries are often defeated due to a lack of field training. Just as military soldiers become stronger as they continually train, spiritual warriors become stronger in Christ when they continually train in the use of his armaments. Then when war breaks out, they are prepared. Because we want our children to succeed, we must be instrumental in providing field training.

Another factor that leads armies into defeat is low morale. Children develop low morale when they become discouraged and when they lack support. Encouragement and support from parents is foundational in the spiritual development of children. Parents have the power to build up or tear down the esteem of their children by what they say to them—words that they will be held accountable for.

It is important for us to help our children understand that it's an honor to put on the armor that God has provided. It is our uniform, and it identifies on which side we fight. It says to the Devil, "I am a child of the King. I am not intimidated by you. I am prepared. My ways are my Father's ways. You are a defeated foe, and because of that knowledge and guarantee I walk in the freedom of faith." The seal of the Holy Spirit is a spiritual covering that signifies four truths: a provision of security, a mark of ownership, a certification of genuineness, and a sign of approval.

Prayer is indispensable to the putting on of God's armor. It will enable our children to have confidence that the armor will protect them. We can be sure that when our children prayerfully and confidently don the arsenal that God has provided, they will never experience defeat.

12

SATAN'S TACTICS: TO STEAL, KILL, AND DESTROY

Your adversary the devil prowls around like a roaring lion, seeking someone to devour.

1 PETER 5:8

Jesus said, "When a strong man, fully armed, guards his own palace, his goods are safe; but when one stronger than he attacks him and overcomes him, he takes away his armor in which he trusted and divides his spoil" (Luke 11:21-22). The "strong man" to whom Jesus referred is us, and the "stronger" man is Satan.

Satan is the ruler of the world system, a fallen angel, and the ruler of the kingdom of the air. But there is good news: even though Satan's purpose is to destroy God's work, Jesus came to destroy the works of the Devil. Furthermore, God created Satan, which means that Satan is in no way God's equal. Though Satan is superior to man in intellect and strength, he is inferior to God in every way. Some people say that Satan is the opposite of God, but God has no opposite. Nothing is even remotely comparable to him. It is common for believers to assign Satan much more power than he actually has and to allow that falsehood to intimidate them. While it is true that *apart from Christ* we are all helpless, we have the power *in Christ* to overcome Satan.

SATAN'S OBJECTIVE

One of the keys to success in spiritual battle is understanding the various tactics that Satan uses against our children. And we must understand those tactics from the perspective of Satan's fundamental goal: to strip them of all their armor. Luke 11:22 says, "when one stronger than he attacks him and overcomes him, he takes away his armor in which he trusted and divides his spoil." In our last chapter we discussed the armor that God has given our children and what each piece represents. Because it covers them from head to toe, Satan wants to steal it from them so they will have a vulnerable place for a direct attack. Consider again what he desires to steal from our children:

- the truth of God's Word (what girds their waists)
- righteousness (their breastplates)
- the gospel of peace (shoes for their feet)
- their faith (their shields)
- their salvation (their helmets)
- the Spirit of God (their swords)
- their prayer life (their ultimate covering)

Satan sees this armor and weapons, and he seeks to neutralize them with devilish tactics. What are the tactics of the Evil One? He uses conflict, doubt, unbelief, and abuse.

UNRESOLVED CONFLICT WITHIN THE HOME

The primary tactic that Satan uses to strip children of their armor is conflict between parents and children, sometimes even resulting in abuse. In doing so he can potentially produce mass casualties for decades to come, in a sense hitting two birds with one stone. Conflict between parents, divorce, abuse, and rejection are just a few primary results of conflict that directly affect a child. Another area is what psychologists refer to as emotional incest.

Emotional incest occurs when a parent is not getting his or her needs met by his or her mate and turns to a child to discuss problems, struggles, and emotions that are meant to be shared with an adult. Parents often do this without realizing it. It occurs most frequently in a divorce or imminent divorce situation. The hurting parent inadvertently elevates the child into the role of the "man" or "woman of the house," giving the child excessive amounts of responsibility as a confidant and even adult household responsibilities. Most children step up to that role, but when the parent remarries, children end up being demoted from being adults to being children again. It is estimated that over 70 percent of second marriages fail due to problems with the children of the first marriage. This can cause all kinds of problems in the home, not to mention in the children, and needs to be guarded against carefully.

Children have a natural tendency to internalize conflict and stressful situations and to assume that whatever has occurred is their fault. As a result, they become consumed with pain, guilt, and shame and inadvertently loosen their armor, making it easy for the enemy to slip it off and devour them.

While it may be true that Satan has the power to kill a believer—though never without permission from God—Satan's goal is usually simply to destroy the believer's personal faith and walk with Christ. Satan knows that if the believer is dead, he has lost, because Scripture promises that if we are absent from the body, we are present with the Lord. Once our bodies are dead, our spirits are escorted to heaven, where Satan no longer has the power to deceive us. Satan would rather wound us, prompting us to turn our backs on God and on other believers. If he can create a wound in a child who has not yet developed the reasoning skills to combat the assault and does not have parents who can stand against the attack on behalf of the child, the hurt and defeat will likely fester for years to come. I know many adult children like this. Although they are in their thirties, forties, and fifties, they are walking through life with wounds filled with gangrene because of childhood hurts. The biggest problem with this is that wounded people wound other people. So if they are married and have children of their own, they are often unwittingly and unconsciously causing damage within their own immediate family and not understanding why.

DOUBT AND UNBELIEF

Another tactic that Satan uses to attack our children is doubt and unbelief. Satan said to Jesus, "If you are the Son of God . . ."

(Matthew 4:3) even though he knew full well that Jesus is indeed the Son of God. He used the word *if* in an attempt to create doubt in our Savior's mind. *If* is a powerful word that Satan often uses. Through this small word, he breeds doubt in the heart of children everywhere. "If you have value, then why do you keep failing?" "Did your parents *really* say . . . ?" We've all seen it occur in our children's lives when we gave them specific directions to do something and they did it a different way, then said, "I thought you said . . ." or "I didn't think you'd mind if . . ." We do the same in our relationship with God and can expect no less from our children. It is natural for the sin nature to minimize or justify its behavior. Learning to take every thought captive is the answer to this common dilemma.

Our children can combat the unbelief in these attacks on their mind with God's Word, just as Jesus did. "The Word of God says . . ." is a powerful weapon, but they can't use it if they don't know God's Word. Remember the cognitive or mental process that we discussed in Chapter 8? We are to teach our children to compare their thoughts to what God's Word says. The most effective cure for unbelief is for our children to take their stand on the Word of God. When the first two tactics of the Devil fail, he will often turn to his old standard: discouragement and distortion.

DISCOURAGEMENT AND DISTORTION

Satan loves to discourage children. Discouragement is one of his most effective tools. When our children fall prey to this tactic, believing the Devil's accusations and suggestions that they are utter failures, they and we end up feeling empty. This sense of emptiness will render them ineffective for Christ by making them feel hopeless, weak, and unable to fight. It will sap them of initiative. But Christ said that they have the power to overcome through him. He is always ready and waiting for them to return to him so that he may strengthen them by his Word.

Satan also loves to twist God's truth. How can our children defend against such a tactic? In banks, new tellers are trained to spot counterfeit money by closely examining real bills. They touch, feel, and learn to recognize genuine currency so that when a counterfeit comes along they are able to spot it immediately. In the same way, training our children for spiritual warfare focuses not primarily on the Devil and his methods but on the genuine power and promises of Christ. Only after knowing the truth can our children spot from afar the Devil's counterfeits.

Satan encourages conflict and abuse. He sows seeds of doubt and unbelief. He discourages children and distorts the truth. In actuality, the tactics of the enemy are endless. Parents will become aware of each of them by knowing God's Word, which exposes Satan's lies. But the knowledge of the Devil's schemes are not enough to ensure victory. We must determine in our hearts never to give up and to teach our children to endure and persevere. When they fail, become difficult or rebellious, reject the truth they've been taught, and go their own way or that of the world, we must take a bigger spiritual burden on as parents and fight on the front lines.

THE REBELLIOUS OR DEFIANT CHILD

Beloved, do not be surprised at the fiery trial when it comes upon you to test you, as though something strange were happening to you. But rejoice insofar as you share Christ's sufferings.

1 PETER 4:12-13

I hate suffering. I especially dislike it when it involves my children because that seems to be much more intense and painful. As a matter of fact, when Satan assaults my children, I take it quite personally. It infuriates me and motivates me to respond, and I become a mother-lioness. Knowing this, Satan often attacks *me* through them. Let me explain.

My twenty-one-year-old son, Paul, is a special-needs adult-child. He is a weak link spiritually—that is, a viable tool for Satan to use and misuse to create unneeded chaos, trial, heartache, and pain in his life and those associated with him, specifically his family. Paul is not a purposeful vessel for the enemy but a helpless one. He is incapable of defending himself and others. As a result, Satan takes great joy in tormenting both my son and me through the agony Paul experiences.

During some of the most spiritually influential work I've done in deliverance ministry on behalf of our Lord, the evil spirit has left the person I'm working with and has gone directly into my helpless son. For example, on one occasion an evil spirit that identified itself as "Suicide" left the woman he had been assaulting, then went into my son. I have then returned home after being on the front lines all day, only to have to work double time spiritually with my son. Satan is ruthless and relentless in his assaults, and to find him relentlessly torturing my son instantly puts me on the front line of battle. I have had to learn how to protect my son spiritually because he cannot do so himself.

During the formative years of Paul's life, he was quite a handful. He had serious behavioral problems in and out of the home. After becoming a believer, I consistently tried to teach him God's ways, but while he could verbally mimic the truth I was teaching him, his behavior manifested grave defiance. Because I wasn't fully aware of his deteriorating mental and emotional state and the illness that was consuming his mind, I addressed Paul's behavior as only a spiritual problem and had no success in helping him.

Well-meaning believers convinced me that Paul needed to go through deliverance, which he did, and when that didn't deter or improve his behavior, medical tests revealed a much more serious issue: my son was schizo-affective, an illness that is hereditary from his paternal family tree. In short, Paul lives in a world void of reality in every form. Twenty-four hours a day he is plagued with auditory and visual hallucinations. As a result, he has great difficulty functioning in society, maintaining appropriate relationships with others, and believing truth.

Paul has no reasoning skills. So encouraging and teaching him to change a behavior is often met with what appears to be defiance, but in reality it is an inability to comprehend the necessity to change. Further, while spiritual warfare seems interesting to him, he's unable to grasp the tools available to him to combat the continual lies he's told by the enemy of his soul and the delusions caused by the lack of natural chemicals in his mind. Because of his inability to reason, accept and apply truth, discern an attack of the enemy, and apply the normal cognitive process, Paul averages about the age of eight emotionally, and he will likely deteriorate further the older he gets and as more psychotic breaks occur.

As a result, Paul's illness continually places me on the front line of battle where I have to go toe-to-toe with the enemy and his evil cohorts. I pray for protection over my son, for God's intervention, wisdom, and guidance, and for the ultimate penetration of my son's heart and soul through the truth of Jesus Christ. I look forward to the day my son and I are in heaven and he's free from this debilitating illness.

While Paul is not purposely rebellious, having a child who is insurgent can cause as much anguish to parents. Proverbs 22:6 haunts such parents and can lead to guilt and condemnation: "Train up a child in the way he should go; even when he is old he will not depart from it." I have been counseling youth for over fifteen years, and I racked my brains for years wondering what I could have done differently. Let me save you some time.

A very wise friend and mentor of mine, Willie Wooten, is the Director of Counseling for Focus on the Family. As I grappled with the problem of guilt and regret, he asked me what seemed like an odd question.

"Leslie, how big is a windshield?" he asked smiling.

"What?" I answered. "What do you mean?" He repeated the question.

"I don't know," I said. "Maybe this big." I spread my arms wide.

"Good," he answered. "And how big is a rearview mirror?"

"It's small, Willie, very small." I was getting frustrated, but out of respect I was willing to answer his questions.

"And what's the rearview mirror for?" he asked.

"To glance at, to make sure you're safe, to see what's behind you, to help you get where you're going."

"That's right," he answered, "and what would happen if all you did when you were driving was stare into the rearview mirror?"

I laughed. "I'd wreck, probably killing myself and everyone else in the process."

"Leslie," he wisely stated, looking into my eyes from across the room, "that rearview mirror is the past, and the windshield is the future. Only look behind you for a second to make sure you're making a wise decision. Don't live in the past or you'll never go forward."

That was a light bulb moment for me. Parents are often inundated with what they have done wrong and how they could have done things better, but as Willie so wisely pointed out, this is not the answer. Focusing on the past will only entrap you in disappointment. Equally so, focusing on the future will only bring fear of the unknown. The answer is focusing on the level of rebellion and the current situations in your child's life that are evident today. Jesus tells us in Matthew 6:34 (NIV), "Therefore do not worry about tomorrow, for tomorrow will worry about itself. Each day has enough trouble of its own."

Perhaps you did make negative decisions during your child's formative years. Acknowledge them, confess them, repent of them, and walk in faith that you've been forgiven. But your child needs you *now*; so focus on this moment in time.

THE REBELLIOUS CHILD

There are different levels of rebellion. Some children are defiant in specific areas of their lives, but through consistent direction, consequences, and encouragement they eventually turn toward doing what is right in God's eyes. Other children hold on to these areas in defiance with their feet dug into the ground no matter what and eventually are faced with natural consequences as adults that force them to change, perhaps being fired from a job or going to jail. The third alternative is the rebellious child who in complete defiance turns his or her back on everything he or she once knew to be true and takes up allegiance with the opposing camp.

In a previous chapter we addressed the necessity of parental warriors' examining whom their child serves in terms of allegiance, relationship, and obedience. The rebellious child serves Satan, not God. I know this is a strong statement, but the Bible tells us we cannot serve two masters—we will hate one and love the other (Matthew 6:24). The child who is sold out to God and God alone has one Master—Jesus Christ (Matthew 23:8).

SALVATION vs. HEART SOFTENING

My son Paul made a profession of faith when he was eight years old. To this day I still have the note he wrote me after that church service telling me that "Jesus saved him" and that he wanted Jesus to help him "choose the right." In the years that followed, I've gone back time and time again to that day he received Jesus into his heart and have read and re-read his awkward handwriting in pencil on the back of a tithing envelope. Was it real? Was it a true conversion? I believe so. Although my son's health began to seriously deteriorate shortly after that, when he was eight he was the healthiest emotionally and mentally. The temptation is to continue to pray for my son's salvation, and while that would cause no damage, I feel it's neither beneficial nor helpful because he's already saved.

I know of people who have gotten "saved" time and time again. The problem with this scenario is that it proclaims unbelief. God's Word tells us that if we profess Jesus as Lord and call on him, we are saved (Joel 2:32). Since we are all sinners, we all rebel against God's ways and inevitably create separation between him and us. That is not a reason to get saved again. Instead, the cure is the confession of our sins through renouncing the lie and receiving God's truth in its place. Repentance comes through the softening of our hearts, humility, and receptivity, and this is how we need to direct our prayers for a rebellious child.

When we pray for our children, the Holy Spirit will reveal, when asked, the specific point to focus on in prayer. He will be your compass and will show you which way to pray. However, there is a standard way of covering the bases with hard-hearted children:

- that their hearts would be softened,
- that conviction would haunt them until they repent,
- that God will do whatever it takes to get their attention,
- that they will recognize their behavior as sin,
- that they will renounce their involvement in this sin.
- that they will receive truth in its place.

In the name of Jesus, on behalf of your child, break the spiritual web of deceit that has entangled your child—rebellion, drugs, alcohol, confusion, or whatever.

TAKING CARE OF SELF

One of the greatest errors made when parents have a rebellious child is not taking care of themselves spiritually. We become consumed with frustration over our children and angry with God for allowing such a thing to occur. Shortly after Paul's eighteenth birthday, I was faced with what appeared to be an insurmountable situation.

Paul is mentally ill and has been tormented with schizophrenia for most of his life. As a mother, it has been devastating to me to watch this talented young man mentally deteriorate over the years. Over a ten-year period of time, he has gone from being a genius (literally—184 IQ) to having the mentality of an eight-year-old. To make matters worse, as I mentioned earlier, he is plagued every moment of every day by auditory and visual hallucinations. Can you imagine never having peace and quiet, never having the ability to distinguish between reality and delusions? As a mother I have rarely felt so helpless. While medication has at times helped Paul's hallucinations diminish, they have never disappeared entirely. As a result, Paul vacillates between suicidal and homicidal inclinations, sometimes experiencing what appears to be a meditative trance, sometimes excessively writing what the voices are telling him in a screenplay format. Unfortunately, these voices mislead him to say and do inappropriate things that jeopardize his safety and the safety of others.

Shortly after his eighteenth birthday Paul had a psychotic break and lost all concept of what little reality he was clinging to. One day he just woke up, dressed himself in a T-shirt, shorts, and flip-flops, and left our home in Colorado without a word to anyone. I was devastated to say the least, aware of his fragile state of mind, fearing the worst. I turned my anger and agony on God. Not only did I bathe in fear and sorrow, I swam laps in it, causing me to remain drenched in pain twenty-four hours a day. The problem wasn't the situation itself, because as a believer I could rely on God to comfort me during this time—if I so chose. The problem was that I am a control freak, and I had no control of the pain and fear I was experiencing, nor did I have control of my son's whereabouts. Suddenly the rubber hit the road in my spiritual walk with God. I knew his Word inside and out, but would I use it in this dire state of mind?

Raised in a dysfunctional home where sex abuse and physical abuse were the norm, I learned to believe the lie that if I could control the circumstances around me, I could protect myself from all aspects of suffering. Although that wasn't really the case, I spent a great deal of energy trying to manipulate situations and those around me as a survival mechanism to minimize the pain I experienced in life. One way I did this was by avoiding intimacy at all costs with everyone, including God. Don't get me wrong—I loved the Lord and spent a great deal of time with him every day, but I always kept him and other important people in my life at arm's length, believing this would increase my chances of avoiding pain.

I called the police, put out a missing-person report on Paul, and put all of his friends and our family on alert in case they miraculously heard from him. I went online and put my son on every prayer list I could find. Then I had to wait in agonizing and relentless pain, every day, one after the other. For hours and hours a day I would wonder, *Is Paul dead or alive? Will he be able to grasp enough reality to remember who he is or where he's from or how to get home or that his mom loves him? Why has God allowed this to happen? What if someone abuses him?* I have never cried more in my life as I grieved the what ifs and whys.

In order to retain my own sanity, I was forced to find some hope to hold on to. God has been so faithful in my life and has never forsaken me; so I instinctively turned to him and his Word. Never in all my life have I ever been so dependent on anything or anyone as I became on God at that time. I knew I'd go off the deep end of sorrow if I loosened my grip on the prayers and promises that kept us connected. I knew that he was not promising me that my son would be returned to me, or even that he would be cared for appropriately for that matter, but he did promise to spend every minute of every day with me as I grieved.

I spent hours upon hours talking to God every day, week after week. I slept very little during the months that followed, my grief and fear waking me and refusing to allow me to rest. But I pressed on, combating the lies the enemy whispered to me in the long, dark hours of the night, and I stood on God's promise to comfort me. It was the hardest thing I've ever gone through. Coming from someone who endured years of abuse as a child, chronic depression that led to multiple suicide attempts, and the loss of several loved ones, that is a significant statement. My children, Charlene and Paul, were my world, and when they suffered, I did too.

After Paul had been gone about five months, I fell on my face in weariness and sorrow. For all those months my prayer had been that the Lord would bring my son home so he could get the care he needed. But now, in complete exhaustion, I could not ask that anymore. Although I began to lose hope, I also knew that the Spirit of God was interceding for me in ways that I was not able to in my weak state. I didn't know what to pray for anymore, but he did (Romans 8:26).

In my fragile state I cried out to God and asked him to at least let me know if Paul was dead or alive. It was okay if God didn't bring him back home. I knew Paul would be in his hands, but I pleaded for him to somehow reveal to me if Paul was alive. I fell asleep on the floor and slept sixteen hours straight, awaking to the peace that surpasses all understanding (Philippians 4:7). I wanted to put a meaning behind that peace. Did it mean that Paul was alive? Did it mean he was in heaven with God? God gave me no clarification at that time, so I was forced to just dwell in the comforting river of peace that was present.

Two weeks later I felt the Holy Spirit prompting me to e-mail Paul at his old Internet address from years before. *Yeah, right! This isn't God speaking,* I thought. *Paul's a homeless schizophrenic who doesn't have a computer!* I argued. *I'm NOT going to e-mail him,* I said in response to the thought. It was a ludicrous thing to do—e-mailing a homeless person. It made no sense whatsoever. Yet for the next two weeks the Holy Spirit kept prompting me to e-mail my son. Every time I refused. Have you ever had a wrestling match with God? Let me save you some time and let you in on a little secret: *he always wins!* At 2:00 one morning I awoke—wide awake—prompted by the Holy Spirit to send Paul an e-mail at that very moment. In frustration I pulled back the covers, got out of bed, went to the computer, and reluctantly sent Paul an e-mail asking him to contact me if he received the message. I typed my phone number and told him to call collect. After I sent the e-mail, I went back to bed.

When I woke up a couple of hours later, I was prompted to check my e-mail. I was ecstatic when I saw a returned e-mail from my son. It was a short note telling me he was on a "spiritual trek for God" and was fulfilling a mission as instructed by the voices. I immediately e-mailed him back and gave him my address and phone number again, instructing him to print my message and take it to the nearest police station. Within an hour I got a call from a New York City police officer who was sitting next to Paul!

I filled the police in on Paul's mental condition, and they said they'd keep him with them and feed and take care of him until I could get him home. If you know New York City at all, this is a miracle in itself. Literally thousands of mentally ill homeless people wander the streets there. Because of that, the police are normally unable to make such accommodations, especially in the winter months. At 10:00 the next evening my son was returned home and was hospitalized so he could get the care he so desperately needed.

Now let me share the rest of this miraculous story. After Paul became somewhat stabilized in the hospital, I asked him how he checked his e-mail and what prompted him to do so. In a brief, sane moment (which I assure you is fleeting and rare), he said he heard a *new* voice in his head—one he'd never heard before. It told him to walk down to Times Square in downtown New York. When he got there, a man had a bench set up with computers on it. The "new voice" he was hearing told him to check his e-mail, and the man gave him permission to do so, thus leading him to contact me and return home to obtain medical care.

During the six months Paul had been gone, he had been hospitalized in several different states. It was obvious to the police and any other person who came across Paul on the street begging for food that he was not in his right mind. One police department even kept him in jail overnight for observation. When Paul first arrived in New York City, he stayed in a homeless shelter for children. When the staff counselor asked if he had any family she could call, he said, "My father was killed in a car accident, my mother was brutally murdered, and I have no siblings." None of this was true. They could tell Paul was mentally ill, but they had no resource for contacting me. God was the only option.

Without a doubt, the "new voice" that Paul had heard prompting him to check his e-mail was the Holy Spirit miraculously answering my prayer. Looking back over the period of time that Paul was gone, I see that in my agony over my son, I was forced to cling to God in ways I never had before. The intimacy I developed with my Father in heaven during that time was something I honestly would never have pursued on my own. Knowing this, God allowed a situation to occur in my life that brought me so much pain and sorrow that I was forced to push through all my self-protective barriers into a level of intimacy with him merely to survive.

For the following fourteen months Paul was in and out of the mental hospital, eventually ending up living in a treatment center for the mentally ill. On January 30, 2004, Paul had another psychotic break and walked away from treatment without notifying anyone. After being gone for five months Paul was returned to me in no less a miraculous way.

The agony and grief that I experienced was devastating when my son was gone, just as it is when our children are in rebellion. But instead of focusing on the what ifs and whys, I tell myself, *You've been here before. God did not leave you or forsake you at those times. Instead, you grew closer to him. You lived through it, and you will survive this too—as long as you cling to God.* I may not always know where my son is, what he's doing, whether he has food, whether he is cold or clothed, or whether he has a place to lay his head, but God does, and I *have* to trust him as I push through the present opposition at hand.

PUSHING THROUGH THE OPPOSITION

When I was pregnant with my oldest child, I couldn't wait to give birth and experience this new life. A month past my due date, the doctors induced labor. I was excited and eager to see the child I'd been carrying for over nine months. They administered a drug called Pitocin. Once it entered my body and I experienced my first contraction, I wasn't so excited about induced labor. Hours later, with contractions a minute apart, I was willing to be pregnant for the rest of my life if only the pain would subside. It seemed like forever before the doctors allowed me to push and my beautiful daughter was born. Naturally, the pain I'd experienced was eventually overshadowed by the beauty of my child and the experience of being a first-time mom.

When my second child was ready to make an appearance, I was a bit more prepared. The pain was still intense, but I knew it would end. I knew that I'd overcome the difficulty of labor and that the reward on the other side would be worth every second of the pain.

Such is the case with spiritual battle. When we're in the middle of it, it seems as if it will never end. The ordeal can be excruciating, and doubt assails our hearts, minds, and spirits. But we must not give up. We must believe and trust in God's Word that if we follow his directions and put on the armor of Christ, we will make it to the other side and see our children walk in freedom. We will be stronger and closer to him because of it.

Spiritual battle offers unique challenges through which we must push. What are these obstacles? One of the greatest is the baggage that we inherit from the generations that have gone before us. We know that baggage as *generational curses*.

GENERATIONAL CURSES

One reason our children have difficulty pushing through the opposition and overcoming attacks in their lives is because of *generational curses*—strongholds that have passed to subsequent generations due to family members' involvement in sin. Another way to regard them is as sinful patterns that have become ingrained in our spiritual blueprints. We all have these curses. They are demonic doorways that others have opened. If we were to draw a generational chart of our family tree that displays strongholds over past generations in our family, it would likely reveal some of the struggles that we or our children may have.

In my own family tree there is a generational history of sexual addiction, alcoholism, bitterness, self-hatred, and pride. Despite this history I was considered the black sheep of my family, not because I struggled with those same sins, but because I brought them into the open and began a process of healing. How ironic it was that my family accepted me when I walked in the generational curses; once I stepped out of them, however, they rejected me. Satan's goal is for these curses to remain unaddressed, because as long as these sins are hidden, our children remain in bondage to them. My greatest joy is to have served as a pioneer for my mother, brothers, and children, leading the way out of the curses that for generations had bound us.

Why are so many believers subject to generational curses even though they have put their faith in Christ for salvation? How do we overcome generational curses?

THE POWER OF UNITED PRAYER

As you ponder the truths in this chapter, take a concrete action step. Find a confidant who will pray with you on your child's behalf—if not your mate, then someone close to your family. Acts 1:14 tells us that there is power in numbers. When we are in agreement with one another and with the truth of God's Word in prayer, we will see answers that amaze us. Matthew 18:20 further makes this point: "For where two or three are gathered in my name, there am I among them."

In my prayer ministry, when I gather with several women who are experiencing an array of problems with their children, we pray for one child at a time, with one person praying aloud while the others in the group are praying silently for the same person. This is a powerful way to pray, tearing down strongholds, claiming territory that was once given over to demonic activity, and empowering the individual to walk in the freedom of Christ.

PRESSING THROUGH

When you grapple with your child's rebellion, think of the Garden of Gethsemane. It was a place of sorrow and trouble—overwhelming to the point of death. It was a place of disappointment, betrayal, and deception. However, it was also a place of prayer, mercy, and a proclamation of God's strength. Jesus pressed through the opposition there and went on to suffer death at the hands of sinful men; then he rose again. Because he pressed through the storm, we now experience the freedom that comes with his victory. Following Jesus our example, we must in a similar manner press through whatever we are experiencing. We must know and believe that freedom lies on the other side of the storm.

14

AGE-APPROPRIATE WARFARE

Simply getting people to go to church regularly is not the key to becoming a mature Christian. Spiritual transformation requires a more extensive investment in one's ability to interpret all life situations in spiritual terms.

GEORGE BARNA,
THE BARNA GROUP

Erik H. Erikson was a research specialist in the field of human development. In his studies he found that everyone is born with a basic blueprint of capabilities and distinct temperaments. According to Erikson, each person passes through eight developmental stages that build one upon the other:

1. Infancy (0-1 year of age)
2. Toddler (1 to 2 years of age)
3. Early Childhood (2 to 6 years of age)
4. Elementary and Middle School Years (6 to 12 years of age)
5. Adolescence (12 to 18 years of age)
6. Young Adulthood (19 to 40 years of age)
7. Middle Adulthood (40 to 65 years of age)
8. Late Adulthood (65 to death)[31]

Erikson believed that each stage is characterized by a different psychological "crisis." That is, the individual must learn the necessary skills of that stage before emotionally and mentally moving on to the next stage. If the person copes with a particular crisis in an unhealthy manner, the outcome will be more struggles with that issue later in life. For example, during the infancy stage children learn trust or mistrust of others. They depend on their caregivers to feed them, give them attention, and keep them warm and clean. If those needs are not met during the first twelve months of development, children will develop mistrust toward people, their environment, and even themselves.

Erikson's research on the development of identity was founded as much in personal experience as in research. His father, an unnamed Danish man, abandoned his mother before he was born. For the first three years of his life, Erikson's Jewish mother raised him alone, until she married Erikson's pediatrician, Dr. Theodor Homburger. Erikson's identity continued to be assaulted by classmates who relentlessly teased the young boy for being a tall, blue-eyed, blond Jew. As a result of his own fragile identity being damaged as a child, Erikson made a career out of exposing the developmental needs of all humans, in an attempt to help us better meet one another's needs as we mature.

Research shows that children grow and change in four dramatic ways: physically, intellectually, emotionally, and socially. If one or more of these areas of the child is not developed, the child does not grow into a healthy, happy adult.

• Physical development is the way a child's body grows.

• Intellectual development involves a child's thinking. Children learn to think by undertaking challenging tasks.

• Emotional growth involves the development of a child's feelings.

• Social development is the way a child learns to work, play, and interact with other people.

There is, however, another area that researchers have identified, and that is moral development—the judgment of the goodness or badness of human action and character. Moral development must not be confused with spiritual development, which is important to examine when teaching a child spiritual warfare.

Moral development can be easily defined as the teaching or exhibiting of goodness or correctness of character and behavior. It is more than simply knowing "right" from "wrong" because morals are often regulated by the world's standard rather than by God's. For example, in the 1920s a woman was thought to be immoral if she wore a bikini in public. Today, by the world's standard, that is acceptable. As the world continues to deteriorate as we approach the Second Coming of Christ, we see more and more gray areas. As believers we live moral lives according to God's standard as outlined in the Word of God, the Bible. The law of God should be our standard for morals, not the ever-changing world.

Spiritual development is less about moral rules and more about intimacy with Jesus, which must be taught in conjunction with biblical morals. Without it, we bypass grace and end up raising legalistic terrors who have lives blanketed in guilt, shame, and self-hatred. Spiritual development by definition has a spiritual nature. In other words, helping your children understand that they are not human beings in a spirit world but spirit beings in a human world will equip them with a correct perspective on life. Next we can help build on that truth by teaching them about who they are in Christ—unique, special, and irreplaceable—and that God has sanctified them (that is, he has set them apart for a spiritual purpose). Spiritual development is crucial and something that you cannot possibly pass on to your children if you have not experienced it yourself.

As I have presented the gospel to the unsaved, I have heard countless people proclaim their righteousness before God from the perspective that they've done more good than bad: if God grades on a curve, these people feel they are certain to get into heaven. But moral goodness does not even register on the same scale as spiritual development, which ultimately affects the soul, intimacy with God, and the supernatural powers associated with God's Word.

SPIRITUAL DEVELOPMENT/MATURITY

Research shows us that a person's moral foundation is generally in place by the time they reach age nine. Their fundamental perspectives on truth, integrity, meaning, justice, morality, and ethics have been formed by this age, and while they will be refined in the years that follow, they become rooted in the heart of children in the first several years of life.

In fact, researcher George Barna concludes that most people's minds are made up and they believe they know what they need to know spiritually by age thirteen. Their focus in absorbing religious teaching after that age is to gain reassurance and confirmation of their existing beliefs rather than to glean new insights that will redefine their foundations.

Research has underscored the importance of families, not churches, taking the lead in the spiritual development of children. "In situations where children became mature Christians we usually found a symbiotic partnership between their parents and their church," Barna pointed out. "The church encouraged parents to prioritize the spiritual development of their children and worked hard to equip them for that challenge. Parents, for their part, raised their children in the context of a faith-based community that provided security, belonging, spiritual and moral education, and accountability. Neither the parents nor the church could have done it alone."

AGE-APPROPRIATE SPIRITUAL WARFARE

When approaching age-appropriate warfare, we must look at it from two perspectives—what we as parents are responsible to do and to teach our children and what, depending on our children's age, is their responsibility. We can intervene on behalf of our children, but as they grow in stature, they can immediately begin to learn warfare based on their age and development. Find the age of your child in the material below, and consider their developmental skills and what they are capable of learning.

When teaching your child warfare, remember that active learning for all ages is fun and captivating; process-oriented; student-based, not teacher-based; and relational. Also, learning requires a child's *active* participation, uses activities and materials that are concrete, real, and relevant to their lives, and includes all senses—sight, hearing, taste, smell, and touch. So include dramas or stories, skits, object lessons, and even experiments when teaching your children. Encourage movement, participation, exploration, hands-on involvement, talking and discussion, and individual and family prayer.

With young children, make sure that activities are short and attention-grabbing. When dramatizing a story from the Bible with small children, focus on the events and the emotional and sensory impact that would have been experienced by the characters in the Bible.

In closing, always try to debrief your children. Reflect on their interpretation of what they learned. How did they feel? What did they learn while doing warfare? What does it mean to them? How will they handle a future situation when attacked? How will doing spiritual warfare change them and help them grow? All these are wonderful things to explore with your children as you teach them.

THE DEVELOPMENTAL CHART

When considering where to start with your children, consider their developmental level as listed below. If your child is a pre-teen and hasn't been raised knowing and participating in spiritual warfare, you may need to start integrating him or her slowly to the concept as outlined in the first few stages below. Also, I have begun this section with a pre-birth stage not mentioned in Erik Erikson's work. This is because research shows that while in the womb, children can perceive the events in the outside world and experience reactions and emotions based on what's going on around them.

PRE-BIRTH STAGE—AGE: CONCEPTION TO NINE MONTHS

If you or your mate are pregnant, you must understand the miracle that has occurred. One out of four hundred million sperm have connected with and penetrated a healthy egg (generally one out of approximately 150). Even when she doesn't know she is pregnant, the woman's body does and stops producing ripened eggs. At the same time, her uterine lining miraculously changes and becomes thicker, thus preparing a healthy, safe place for the baby to grow.

Over the next few weeks, thousands of genes connect and work together to form the baby's physical characteristics—sex, eye color, diseases, handicaps, immune system. Cells divide, and the amniotic sac develops. Another cluster becomes the placenta, and within six weeks the baby is an embryo. The baby has a neck, a head with rudimentary eyes and ears, a brain, and a beating heart. The baby also has a bloodstream, a digestive system, kidneys, a liver, and tiny buds that will become arms and legs. God is knitting the baby together (Psalm 139:13-16).

The spine develops, and within another week the baby has nostrils, lips, and a tongue. The first teeth have even started to develop. What were buds a week ago are now arms and legs. Within a month, organs and features are complete, but the baby will continue to mature until he or she reaches the stage where the baby is ready to make an entrance into the world.

I am sharing these prenatal stages of development so you can recognize how your baby is growing and will know how to pray. It is important to pray throughout this process because one out of three fetuses does not make it thus far due to miscarriage. We must not forget the assault that was made on our Savior's life after his conception. Satan is no respecter of persons. He does not want a child born into a Christian home to godly parents. Remember, he has no sympathy or empathy for the fact that this is a helpless child. He is ruthless, and parents must pray through these stages of development with the surety that the Lord is intervening in ways we cannot see.

STAGE 1: INFANCY—UP TO AGE ONE

During this stage of development, newborns depend on their guardians for everything—food, warmth, and affection. Based on whether or not their needs are met, they learn to trust or mistrust others, their environment, and themselves. Thus it is essential that we focus on building that trust by meeting their physical needs. In doing so, our children learn that we are there for them and that they can trust us in other areas.

Within the first year of life, the death rate for children is one in

141, and in the following three years one in 2,941. Historically, the top causes of death are:

• Accidents, including automobile accidents, whiplash, drowning, falls, sports injuries, burns, machinery accidents, suffocation, natural accidents, accidental eye injury, toy-related injuries, and occupational injuries[32]

- Congenital defects including chromosome conditions
- Cancer
- Homicide
- Heart disease
- Influenza and pneumonia
- Perinatal conditions
- Septicemia
- Non-malignant cancers
- Chronic lower respiratory diseases
- Other causes such as SIDS (Sudden Infant Death Syndrome)

So we can see that childhood deaths in the first four years of life involve physical illnesses and accidents. We need to pray against both these areas in our children's lives.

The first year of your children's lives can be a wonderful time to introduce spiritual warfare by beginning to involve them in prayer and physical activity. They can hold on to objects and begin to attain eye to hand coordination. Talk with them openly about the Lord, so they become familiar with his name and promises.

STAGE 2: TODDLER—AGE ONE TO TWO

During the first year of life, newborns come to the false understanding that the world revolves around them. They cry, and they get a need met; they coo, and people pay attention; they make a sound, and everyone focuses on them. During the second stage of development, these same children are learning that there is more to their world. As toddlers, they learn to walk, talk, use the bathroom, and do other things for themselves. It's a time of detaching somewhat from the parental figures and developing some independence. Through this newfound freedom, they are learning about themselves.

If parents encourage their children's use of initiative and reassure them when they make mistakes, children will develop the confidence needed to cope with future situations that require choice, control, and independence. If parents are overprotective or disapproving of children's acts of independence, children may begin to feel ashamed of their behavior or have too much doubt of their abilities.

Teaching your children warfare during the second stage of their lives is most enjoyable. My grandson, Jonathan, is two, and I read and re-read biblical stories to him, pray with and for him, and buy him activities that promote spiritual activities. I recently bought him a sword and some "armor" for him to play with, and I talk with him about defending himself spiritually. While much of what I say is over his head, I am planting seeds in his young heart.

STAGE 3: EARLY CHILDHOOD—AGE TWO TO SIX

Children have newfound power at this stage as they develop motor skills and become more and more engaged in social interaction with people around them. They now must learn to achieve a balance between eagerness for more adventure and more responsibility and learning to control impulses and childish fantasies.

If parents are encouraging but consistent in discipline, children will learn to accept without guilt that certain things are not allowed but at the same time will not feel shame when using their imagination and engaging in make-believe role-plays. If this balance is not preserved, children may develop a sense of guilt and may come to believe that it's wrong to be independent.

This is an important age for our children to be equipped to pray for themselves. They are naturally going to become more and more independent; so begin to teach them how to recognize the need for prayer and in what circumstances. Also help them accept the Bible as their source for truth. Do not feed them fairy tales but rather the truth found in God's Word. Encourage them through creative means to draw, act out, or participate in storytelling. This is a good age to start educating them about God's armor and how it's used.

STAGE 4: ELEMENTARY AND MIDDLE SCHOOL YEARS— AGE SIX TO TWELVE

School is the important event at this stage. Children learn to make things, use tools, and acquire the skills to be workers and potential providers. And they do all these while making the transition from the world of home into the world of peers.

If children can discover pleasure in intellectual stimulation, being productive, and seeking success, they will develop a sense of competence. If not, they will develop a sense of inferiority.

At this age more than any other, we need to affirm our children's identity of who they are in Christ and what a miracle they are and what a blessing to us as parents. We can further stimulate their creativity through encouraging them and teaching them to intercede on behalf of others and to document the outcome. I know a lot of powerful prayer warriors in this age group.

I encourage parents to equip their children at this age to share the gospel with their friends and others. They have great potential to reach their friends. This age group reads well and are developing strong reasoning skills. If your children do not have a strong foundation in Jesus Christ at this age, it is more difficult to penetrate their hearts.

STAGE 5: ADOLESCENCE—AGE TWELVE TO EIGHTEEN

We must consider issues of identity versus role confusion. This is the time when young people begin to ask the question, "Who am I?" To successfully answer this question, Erikson suggests, adolescents must integrate the healthy resolution of all earlier conflicts. Did they develop a basic sense of trust? Do they have a strong sense of independence and competence—do they feel in control of their lives? Adolescents who have successfully dealt with earlier conflicts are ready for an identity crisis, which Erikson considers to be the single most significant conflict a person must face.

If the adolescent solves this conflict successfully, he will come out of this stage with a strong identity and will be ready to plan for the future. If not, the adolescent will sink into confusion, unable to make decisions and choices, especially about vocation, sexual orientation, and his role in life in general.

By the time your children have reached this age, they are independent enough to actively do spiritual warfare on their own and to teach others. Parents of this age group are more like mentors than parents. You watch them, interact with them, and help guide them as they struggle through the adult-child phase of life.

STAGE 6: YOUNG ADULTHOOD—AGE NINETEEN TO FORTY

In this stage the most important events are love relationships. No matter how successful you are with your work, said Erikson, you are not developmentally complete until you are capable of intimacy. An individual who has not developed a sense of identity usually will fear a committed relationship and may retreat into isolation.

Adult individuals can form close relationships and share with others if they have achieved a sense of identity. If not, they will fear commitment and will feel isolated and unable to depend on anybody in the world.

Both of my children are currently in this phase of life. One has married and has children of her own. It is important for parents to pray (hopefully you already have been) for your child's lifelong partner. This is also a wonderful time for you as potential grandparents to start the process of praying for your future grandchildren. What a wonderful opportunity you have before you!

CONCLUSION

As believers we all are in the midst of a spiritual battle for the spiritual welfare of our children. Each child has tremendous opportunity to grow in Christ and to serve God faithfully and fruitfully, but each child must also learn the principles of spiritual warfare given to us in the pages of Scripture.

THE POTENTIAL OF A CHILD

King Josiah is perhaps the most memorable example of a child-warrior. Of no other king is it said that "he did not turn aside to the right or to the left" (2 Kings 22:2). Josiah kept his eye on God and reigned for thirty-one years under the favor of his Heavenly Father.

Josiah was only eight years of age when placed upon the throne. What could one expect from a child? Although he was nurtured under an ungodly father, Amon, the young Josiah sought to follow the God of David. This is because children naturally have an inclination toward God at birth.

As life opened to him, Josiah consciously dedicated himself to the service of God. He remembered his Creator in the days of his youth. In the eighth year of his reign he sought and found the Lord, and four years later, when he was twenty years of age, he began to chase idolatry out of the land, seeking to purge the land of the abominations that had polluted it. Thereafter his reign was characterized by close attention to the written Word of God. His ardent religious zeal was not a sudden transitory flash but a bright and steady flame. For six years he labored at his sacred task to overthrow pagan worship and rites. His work of reformation was not entrusted to others. Josiah himself went through the kingdom to see that his commands were executed.

Josiah sought to establish real godliness in the nation and did everything in his power to see it implemented. It would be easy to dismiss a child from any real spiritual responsibility, but I want to encourage you as parents not to limit your children or what God can do through them. We are in the last days, and the children born in this day and time who are walking with Christ have extraordinary strength. With direction from godly parents, God will accomplish amazing feats through them on behalf of his kingdom.

In closing, allow me to encourage you as one parent to another. Parenting is difficult and will remain so long after we become empty-nesters. As our children grow and mature in their humanity and spirituality, their needs shift, and our role changes. We become spiritual mentors, counselors, advisors, and in some unique way that only God has ordained and orchestrated, we still remain connected as their mother or father. So many parents experience the modification in their relationship and get scared, desperately hanging on to their children in an attempt to maintain their parental role, but it's inevitable that change occurs in a healthy relationship. Thus it is our responsibility to equip our children for such times, allowing them to mature, change, make mistakes, and celebrate their triumphs, and to encourage their spiritual growth. Teaching them spiritual warfare when they are young is the best way to empower them to conquer life's problems. Learning who they are in Christ, the power and tools accessible to them through him, and how to use them should not be underestimated.

So often children are seen as commodities opposed to the cherished blessing that God intended them to be for us, a part of the fulfillment of his will. We graduate from high school, go to college, get married, and have children because we think that is what we are supposed to do. Then we spend eighteen years longing for an empty nest. Cherish every day you have with your children, equipping, empowering, and encouraging them in Christ. You will make mistakes along the way, I assure you, but with the Lord as the Captain of your vessel, you will not fall down and stay down but will rise to the calling of parenthood, knowing that the ultimate Father has gone before you to pave the way.

Every day of your children's lives remember that they are on loan to you, given as gifts to teach and from whom to learn. Give them back to the Lord daily in your own prayer time. Ask him how to parent your children, recognizing that he will pick up the slack where you fail. He knows you won't be perfect, but he has trusted you with them anyway.

Most of all, give them the best gift you can—the gift of Jesus Christ.

NOTES

1. U.S. GAO, 2002, National Center for Education Statistics, High School Completion, Intercultural Development Research Association, Statistics and Data on Dropout Prevention.
2. National Center for Injury Prevention and Control, Suicide: Fact Sheet, Youth.
3. Frontline, Juvenile Justice, Basic Statistics, Juvenile Arrests; http://ojjdp.ncjrs.org/ojstatbb.
4. Rebecca A. Maynard, *Kids Having Kids*, Robin Hood Foundation.
5. Associated Press report, "Justice: Youth Imprisonment Doubles," *The New York Times*, February 27, 2000.
6. *Substance Abuse: The Nation's Number One Health Problem*, National Survey of Substance Abuse Attitudes, February 2001.
7. National Institute on Drug Abuse (NIDA), U.S. Department of Health and Human Services, February 27, 2006.
8. J. Briere and E. Gil, "Self-Mutilation in Clinical and General Population Samples," *American Journal of Orthopsychiatry*, October 1998: pp. 609-620.
9. H. Barbaree, S. Hudson, and M. Seto, "Sexual Assault in Society: The Role of the Juvenile Offender," in H. Barbaree, W. Marshall, and S. Hudson (editors), *The Juvenile Sex Offender* (New York: The Guilford Press, 1993), pp. 10-11.
10. M. Sickmund, H. Snyder, E. Poe-Yamagata, "Juvenile Offenders and Victims: 1997 Update on Violence," Office of Juvenile Justice and Delinquency, Washington, D.C., 1997.
11. Barna Research Group, "Teenagers," 2002.
12. Federal Reserve Board, 1995 Survey of Consumer Finance, National Adoption Information Clearinghouse, a service of the U.S. Administration for Children and Families, 1999.
13. *Divorce* Magazine, U.S. Divorce Statistics.
14. U.S. Dept. of Health & Human Services, Bureau of the Census, DAD of Tennessee.
15. U.S. Dept. of Health & Human Services, New Hampshire Center for Health Statistics, Survey on Child Health, Washington, D.C., 1993.
16. Centers for Disease Control, "Right Media Strategy," Senate Bill 551, Friendly Shared Parenting Act.

17. U.S. Dept. of Justice, Special Report, September 1988.

18. Centers for Disease Control.

19. *Criminal Justice Behavior*, Vol. 14, 1978, pp. 403-426.

20. National Principals Association Report on the State of High Schools.

21. Rainbows for All God's Children.

22. Fulton County Georgia jail populations, Texas Dept. of Corrections, 1992.

23. Jean Beth Elshtain, "Family Matters: The Plight of American Children," *The Christian Century* (July 1993), pp. 14-21.

24. U.S. Department of Health and Human Services, New Hampshire Center for Health Statistics, Survey on Child Health, Washington, D.C., 1993.

25. David A. Brent, *Journal of the American Academy of Child and Adolescent Psychiatry*, 34 (1995): 209-215.

26. ANRED (Anorexia Nervosa and Related Eating Disorders, Inc.), 2002.

27. See Neil T. Anderson, Terry E. Zuehlke, and Julianne S. Zuehlke, *Christ-Centered Therapy* (Grand Rapids, MI: Zondervan, 2000).

28. Developmental Stages for Children/Youth, Colorado State University, 2004.

29. See Anderson, T. Zuehlke, and J. Zuehlke, *Christ-Centered Therapy*.

30. *Smith Wigglesworth: The Complete Collection of His Life Teachings*, Roberts Liardon, compiler (Tulsa: Harrison House, 1997).

31. (Boston: Free Software Foundation, 2000, 2001, 2002), GNU Free Documentation License, Version 1.2, November 2002.

32. CDC (Centers for Disease Control), NVSR (National Vital Statistics Reports), 2001; www.wrongdiagnosis.com/death/child.

If you would like to contact the author, you can reach her in the following ways:

By letter:
Leslie Montgomery
c/o Dianne Andrews
506 N.W. 6th Street
Ontario, OR 97914

By e-mail:
princesswarrior@lesliemontgomery.com

Via the Internet:
www.lesliemontgomery.com